FOUL DEEDS & SUSPICIOUS DEATHS IN & AROUND COLCHESTER

Wh 4 1. 00

FOUL DEEDS AND SUSPICIOUS DEATHS Series

Foul Deeds and Suspicious Deaths series explores in detail crimes of passion, brutal murders, grisly deeds and foul misdemeanours. From Victorian street crime, to more modern murder where passion, jealousy, or social depravation brought unexpected violence to those involved. From mysterious death to murder and manslaughter, the books are a fascinating insight into not only those whose lives are forever captured by the suffering they endured, but also into the society that moulded and shaped their lives. Each book takes you on a journey into the darker and unknown side of the area.

Other titles in the series

Please contact us via any of the methods below for more information or a catalogue.
WHARNCLIFFE BOOKS
47 Church Street – Barnsley – South Yorkshire – S70 2AS
Tel: 01226 734555 – 734222 Fax: 01226 724438
E-mail: enquiries@pen-and-sword.co.uk - Website: www.wharncliffebooks.co.uk

Foul Deeds & Suspicious Deaths In & Around
COLCHESTER

PATRICK DENNEY

Series Editor
Brian Elliott

Wharncliffe Books

Dedication

To Betty, Larry and family in Cork

First published in Great Britain in 2005 by
Wharncliffe Books
An imprint of
Pen & Sword Books Ltd
47 Church Street
Barnsley
South Yorkshire
S70 2AS

Copyright © Patrick Denney, 2005

ISBN (1-903425-80-8)

Typeset in 11/13pt Plantin by Andy Hemingway, Barnsley.

Printed and bound in England
By CPI UK

Pen & Sword Books Ltd incorporates the Imprints of
Pen & Sword Aviation, Pen & Sword Maritime,
Pen & Sword Military, Wharncliffe Local History,
Pen & Sword Select, Pen & Sword Military Classics
and Leo Cooper.

For a complete list of Pen & Sword titles please contact
PEN & SWORD BOOKS LIMITED
47 Church Street
Barnsley
South Yorkshire
S70 2AS
England
E-mail: enquiries@pen-and-sword.co.uk
Website: www.pen-and-sword.co.uk

Contents

Acknowledgements

I am indebted to a number of people who have provided valuable information and assistance in support of the publication of this book. In particular, I should like to thank Jess Jephcott for information received concerning the various inns and taverns of the town, and for permission to include a number of archive photographs from his private collection. Also to Don Budds for permission to include most of the information contained in Chapter 5. To the Essex Police Museum for permission to include photographic material in their possession, and likewise to the Fordham Local History Society, the Fingringhoe Historical Recorders Group and Colchester Archaeological Trust. To Brian Light for help in producing the location map and to Christopher Doorne for his valued help in unearthing some of the foundation research material.

Finally, I should like to thank the following persons for their individual contributions: Daphne Allen, Marlene Boyle, Philip Crummy, Bryan Drane, Maureen Evans, Peter Evans, John Hedges, Horatio Hunnable, Jenny Kay, John Norman, Janet Read, Richard Shackle, Dave Tate, Reg Totterdell, Alf Wakeling, Sarah Ward and Sandra Yeomans.

If I have made any omissions, it is with regret, and in no way intentional.

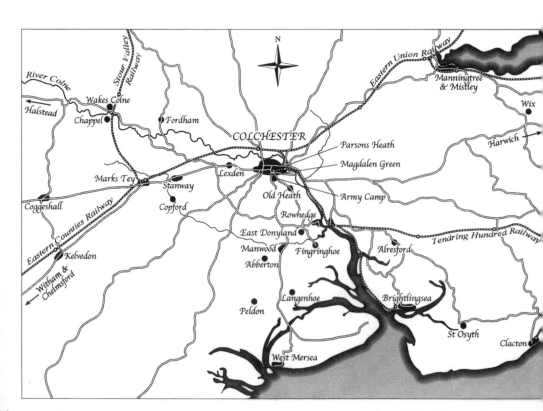

Introduction

Colchester's past has... been peppered with examples of shocking crime...

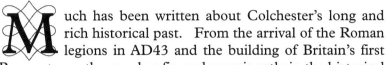uch has been written about Colchester's long and rich historical past. From the arrival of the Roman legions in AD43 and the building of Britain's first Roman town, the area has figured prominently in the historical record. In the main the resulting narratives have tended to emphasise the achievements of the town and its citizens, and rightly so, although one or two of the town's more desperate encounters, such as the infamous Marian persecutions and the plague years of the seventeenth century have also been aired. But like any community, Colchester's past has also been peppered with examples of shocking crime, murder, torture, executions and other events which some may prefer not to dwell on.

It is these so called darker episodes of life, however, which provide the basis for this present volume. Our sinister journey will in fact begin in the sixteenth century when, perhaps, some of the most 'Foul Deeds' of all time were committed against a small band of hapless individuals who dared to contradict such things as the teachings of the Roman church. We will then move on to examine a whole range of ghastly encounters which took place from the eighteenth century onwards. It is perhaps worth noting at this juncture that the subject matter of the book is not confined wholly to the deeds of murderers and other villains (although they appear in plenty), but it is also about the various atrocities and vengeful acts committed by those in positions of authority, whose remit was to administer justice in the name of law and order. And, of course, not all deaths or injuries, suspicious or otherwise, are the result of some dastardly, premeditated crime. Many are the result of some totally unforeseen, and in some cases, bizarre string of events which could befall any one of us. This, of course, has always been the case and brings to mind the well known words of King Solomon regarding time and unforeseen occurrences befalling all men.

In many respects the period covered has been predetermined by the survival and availability of sufficient source material. For example, very few Assize records for Essex have survived from before the sixteenth century, and it was not until the middle of the eighteenth century that we find extensive reporting of crime in local newspapers. This is not to say, however, that the historical record is totally silent for the earlier period. In fact, according to the archaeological record, some of the earliest known examples of criminal acts, or indeed acts of foul play, known to have occurred in the area, date from the early Roman period. For example, dramatic evidence of summary executions, or perhaps even ritual killings, has been uncovered during excavations at Balkerne Lane in the 1970s. A number of human skulls and other body parts were found in the backfill material of a ditch belonging to the former Roman legionary fortress. Several of the skulls recovered showed signs of violent decapitation and the fact that none of the bodies were afforded a decent burial strongly suggests that these may have been the results of criminal executions. The preponderance of human skulls in relation to the number of other body parts may also suggest that it was normal practice to exhibit the heads of those executed on poles at the gate of the town.

All of the corpses, with perhaps just one exception, were of males – although it remains unclear as to whether they were the remains of native Britons, or disgraced Roman soldiers. We know that beheading was common in Roman Britain and that the practice was especially reserved for the better class of criminals – such as Roman citizens, although equally, and despite some laws to the contrary, ritual killings of a religious nature, including the mutilation of body parts after death, was still taking place and a connection in this regard cannot be totally discarded. Whatever the reason for the beheading of the individuals concerned, the heads or other body parts would have been put on public display until such a time as the fleshy parts had begun to decay. Once this had happened the remains would simply have been cast to one side and, finally, haphazardly buried among other refuse and animal matter in any convenient pit or ditch.

Although the Romans may have favoured beheading as a

form of execution, hanging was later to become the accepted form of capital punishment in Britain, although there were exceptions to the rule. Depending upon the nature and seriousness of the crime other means of execution including being pressed to death, burnt at the stake and hanged, drawn and quartered were also commonplace. It is also perhaps worth noting that in former times, especially during the latter years of the eighteenth century, the number of capital offences had risen to over 200, and included such seemingly minor offences as stealing a pocket handkerchief, shoplifting and shooting a rabbit. By 1861, however, the number of such offences had been reduced to just four - murder, High Treason, Arson in a Royal Dockyard and Piracy.

With regard to the scope of the present study, and in particular the geographical coverage, this has been limited to Colchester itself and the surrounding area to a radius of about twelve miles. As far as the content is concerned, the bulk of the material included is from the nineteenth century and is examined through a number of individual cases – mostly criminal in content and involving various acts of violence leading to the death of the victim. The reader will also note numerous points of similarity between the various cases chosen for discussion – the type of crime, method, motive and especially the fact that the majority of crimes were committed by someone who was known to the victim, as opposed to a complete stranger.

Finally, a few words regarding the basic content of the subject matter being discussed. The very nature of a book of this type means that some of the details included may at times prove painful to read. I have thus endeavoured, so far as it is reasonably practicable, to avoid the inclusion of such material which is considered too extreme or distasteful. Neither has it been the intention to glorify, or in any way condone, any of the crimes or incidents referred to. In fact, from a research point of view, it has had the opposite affect. For after having spent hours sifting through reams of evidence, and reading through explicit court cases and coroner's reports, it tends to make you feel very satisfied with one's lot in life and extremely grateful for good health and freedom.

CHAPTER 1

Hanged, Drawn and Quartered
1557

...another one of the bailiffs... dragged him back to the sled and proceeded to hack off his head with a blunt cleaver...

The process of hanging, drawing and quartering was the ultimate punishment in English law for men found guilty of High Treason – women were instead burnt at the stake. This was surely one of the most brutal forms of execution ever invented and was used by Edward I (Longshanks) as a means of dispatching William Wallace of Scotland in 1305.

The full sentence required that the individual be drawn upon a hurdle (similar to a piece of wooden fencing) to the place of execution and then hanged by the neck in the normal way (ie without a drop) so as to ensure that the neck was not broken. Whilst still alive the prisoner's body would then be taken down and his private parts cut off and his stomach slit open. His intestines and heart were then removed and burnt before his eyes (one, of course, would hope that by this time the poor individual was either already dead or had lapsed into a state of unconsciousness!). Next, his head would be cut off and his body divided into four quarters. Finally, the dismembered body parts would be parboiled to prevent them from rotting too quickly and then displayed in a prominent place (the head on a pole) as a warning to like-minded others.

Such was the punishment meted out to a Colchester preacher and tailor named George Eagles (nicknamed Trudgeover or Trudgeover-the-world) in 1557. George had been caught up in the anti-Protestant fervour which had been sweeping the country following the accession to the throne of the Catholic Queen Mary Tudor. This was indeed a terrible time for those of the Protestant faith as she set about trying to restore the country to Catholic Rome. First to be disposed were the Protestant bishops, including the likes of Latimer and

Ridley who were both burnt at the stake, followed by the restoration of Popish rites and imagery in the churches, before finally embarking upon a fanatical crusade of religious persecution against anyone who refused to accept the teachings and doctrines of the Roman Church. During a three year period from 1555 – 1557 more than 300 Protestants nationwide were burnt at the stake – including over seventy from Essex.

Colchester at this time was a medium-sized community with a population of about 5,000. Most of the inhabitants lived in cramped conditions within the confines of the old town wall, although the ancient borough extended well beyond these limits. The town was well known for its cloth-making industry and, almost equally so, for its religious tolerance – particularly with regard to non-conformity. The townsfolk had readily accepted the principles of reform during the reign of Mary's father, Henry, but now their allegiance was once again to be put to the test with her own accession, and demands for a reversal to Catholicism. The majority, of course, when faced with serious persecution, or even the threat of death, quickly recanted their new found beliefs and returned to their former Catholic ways, but some of the more steadfast supporters of the Reformation stood their ground and refused to be intimidated. From the authorities' standpoint they were regarded as rebels and needed to be brought into line. By 1555 the problem locally had intensified and the town was being described as 'a harbourer of heretics' and 'full of rebels.'

George Eagles was one of that number, but unlike the majority of rebels to Catholicism, who were condemned as heretics, he alone was indicted for treason - simply because he had prayed that God would 'turn Queen Mary's heart, or take her away.' This had been construed as an attack on the Queen herself and wishing her personal harm. In reality, of course, he had simply been praying for her own reformation from what he considered to be an apostasy from true Christian worship.

As to what happened next, and in particular the events which led up to his capture and subsequent trial and execution, we must refer to the writings of John Foxe, one of the great Protestant propagandists of the period and the author of the well-known *Book of Christian Martyrs*. According to Foxe, George Eagles had begun his preaching work during the reign of Edward VI, and by the time of the Marian persecutions had become a seasoned preacher and a great encouragement to others. Little is known of his origins other than that he was a man of little formal learning and a tailor by profession. He was, however, obviously inspired with the gift of preaching and travelled widely seeking to spread his gospel message (hence his nickname Trudgeover-the-world) before finally seeking some form of refuge in and around the district of Colchester. Here he managed to keep one step ahead of the authorities, stealthily preaching by day and remaining hidden by night, often sleeping rough in the various woods and heaths which surrounded the town, breaking cover only in times of necessity.

At length, a determined effort was made by the authorities to apprehend him and bring him to justice. A reward of £20 (about £5,000 in today's money) was offered as an enticement for his capture – dead or alive. And with so many 'spies' now seeking him out he was finally spotted, purely by chance, whilst attending a fair on Magdalen Green. Although he managed to give his pursuers the slip, he was followed by a large mob who almost succeeded in catching him. However, in an attempt to throw them off the scent George had managed to conceal himself in a cornfield and had remained there quietly hidden

St Mary Magdalen church from an eighteenth century engraving. The church stood on the north side of Magdalen Green from where George Eagles was spotted whilst attending a fair. The building was demolished in 1852 and a new church erected in 1854 (since demolished). Author's collection

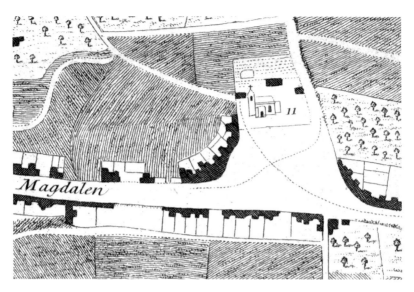

A detail from an eighteenth century town plan showing St Mary Magdalen church standing on the north side of Magdalen Green. Author's collection

until he was sure that his enemies had given up the chase. However, one crafty individual had decided to remain behind and, after climbing a tall tree, kept a silent watch over the area to see whether their quarry would reveal his hiding place. After some time had elapsed, and when the crowd had apparently dispersed, Eagles felt it was safe to emerge from his hiding place only to be spotted by this lone pursuer who quickly descended from the tree and apprehended him.

George was taken into Colchester where he was imprisoned for four days before being sent to Chelmsford, and then on to London where he was brought before the Bishop and other churchmen. He was finally returned to Chelmsford to appear before the sessions where he was indicted and accused of treason, on the grounds that he had been responsible for gathering together companies of men and women contrary to the laws pertaining to acts of sedition. At length he was brought to trial where he attempted to defend himself and made a full declaration of his religion and faith before the judges. However, the charge of treason was upheld and his trial began as follows:

George Eagles, thou are indicted by the name of George Eagles, otherwise Trudgeover-the-world, for that thou didst on such a day make thy prayer that God should turn Queen Mary's heart or else take her away.

He denied that he prayed that God should take her away, but confessed to praying that God would turn her heart in his prayer.

He was thus condemned as a traitor, although on the basis of religion. With the trial over he was carried to the *Crown Inn* in Chelmsford, where a few individuals there tried to get him to confess that he had offended the Queen, and to ask for her forgiveness. In the process of time he was tied up, and with just a psalm book in his hand, was laid upon a hurdle and drawn to the place of his execution. When they arrived at the gallows they proceeded to hang him. After he had been hanging for just a short while the rope was cut by one of the bailiffs and he fell to the ground whilst still alive. At this time another one of the bailiffs, a man named William Swallow, dragged him back to the sled and proceeded to hack off his head with a blunt cleaver (similar to that which might be used in any ordinary household), hitting his neck and chin several times in the process. He then opened him up and plucked out his heart and intestines. The body was then divided into four parts and his bowels burnt. During all of this time – whilst still conscious at any rate – the poor man had remained steadfast, calling upon his Saviour to the end.

His dismembered body parts were then conveyed to the home of the said William Swallow where they were laid upon the fish stalls outside his house, until a horse could be got ready to carry his quarters to their final destinations – one to Colchester, and the others to Harwich, Chelmsford and St Rouses. The quarter which was sent to Colchester was probably put on display in the market place outside the Moot Hall and would, no doubt, have served as a grisly deterrent to others who were of the Protestant persuasion. His head was kept in Chelmsford where it was fixed to a pole at the Market Cross until such time as it was blown down by the wind. After lying in the street for several days, being kicked about in the dirt, it was finally buried in the churchyard during the hours of darkness.

By way of a postscript to this sorry affair it might be of interest to know that this medieval form of punishment remained on the statute books until as late as 1870, although the last recorded act of actually hanging, drawing and quartering somebody took place in 1782. In 1798, and on three further occasions during the nineteenth century, the sentence was only partially completed – ie the victims were hanged and beheaded, but not quartered. Also, with regard to the precise meaning of the words 'hanged, drawn and quartered', there is still some confusion among historians as to what was meant by the term – 'drawn'. For example, did it refer to the process of drawing the sled to the place of execution, or to the act of drawing out the intestines after hanging? Some commentators, for instance, believe that the correct wording of the sentence should in fact be 'Drawn, Hanged and Quartered', emphasising that it refers to the mode of conveyance to the place of execution. One would assume, however, that where the word 'drawn' is placed after the word 'hanged', then it would seemingly refer to the act of disembowelment.

Finally, one can only presume that our forebears must have been made of much sterner stuff than their modern counterparts. For example, can you imagine one of our own local court officials calmly stepping into the breach and proceeding to disembowel somebody, and then to hack off their head and cut their body into pieces.

John Speed's plan of Colchester, published in 1610. Note the location of 'Mary Magdelins' church at the east end of Maudlyne Street. Author's collection

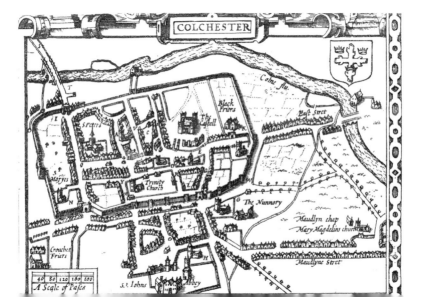

CHAPTER 2

A Deadly Secret
1788

What really happened… will perhaps never be known.

How good are you at keeping a secret? In particular, the kind of secret that could possibly land you in serious trouble, should the truth ever be known. Well such was the dilemma facing a Colchester man named Charles Williams who as an eighteen-year-old in January 1788, had been party to a vicious act of violence which had resulted in the loss of a man's life. Amazingly, he had managed to keep his deadly secret safe from family and friends for over thirty years without revealing so much as a hint as to his involvement in the terrible crime. Finally, however, and as he was approaching the age of fifty, he decided to unburden himself of his guilt and blurted out the truth of the matter to a drinking companion in a local bar. Whether this had been because his conscience had been pricking him as he moved towards old age, or whether the strain of forever being on guard lest he might let something slip in a moment of weakness, had finally proved too much for him, we will never know. It could even, of course, have simply been an act of bravado or a desire to impress his friend. But this simple confession, made at a time when he had probably swallowed one too many, was to result in one of the most talked about cases in the town during the early 1820s. The result was that thirty-five years after the crime had been committed, Charles Williams was arrested on suspicion of murder and brought before a Judge and Jury at the Essex Lent Assize to face the justice of the law.

The victim of the crime, which was committed back in January 1788, was a man named Daniel Holt, a fifty-five-year -old miller from Lexden. Mr Holt had apparently gone off to work at the mill one morning as usual but then failed to return home in the evening as expected. Even so, his family and friends were not unduly troubled as he was in the habit of working late, and perhaps he had even decided to go for a drink after work. He was apparently well-known in the area and would often meet up with friends and acquaintances in the various inns and taverns of the town. Even when he failed to show up for work the following morning nobody was overly concerned - perhaps he had been drinking heavily the night before and was sleeping it off somewhere. However, when he had failed to make an appearance that evening, and then was still missing on the third day, his family and friends finally began to get worried and reported him missing. They searched for him throughout the district but could find no trace of him – that is until two weeks later when a man's body was hauled out of the River Colne by a fisherman in the parish of East Donyland. The body, which was later identified as being that of Daniel Holt, was examined by surgeons from the hospital and although seen to contain some injuries to the head, which may have been caused subsequent to the body entering the water, no evidence was found to suggest foul play, and the coroner's jury had returned a verdict of Accidental Death.

And there the matter was laid to rest and for the most part soon forgotten – that is until once again it became the centre of local gossip and rumour some thirty years later. By this time, of course, about half of the population that was living at the time of the tragedy had passed away and the event was, at best, a distant memory in the minds of those still living. However, for one particular person the events surrounding Mr Holt's death were still crystal clear, despite the passage of time. This person was Charles Williams, the man who was now standing in the dock accused of his murder. And the only reason why Williams was in this perilous position was due to his own confession, when he admitted being involved in the crime, to a drinking acquaintance named William Lester. Mr Lester, of course, was now the principal witness for the prosecution in the proceedings and went on to relate to the court the circumstances of the evening when the prisoner first spoke of his involvement in Mr Holt's murder:

I have known the prisoner for twenty years. We lived about half a mile apart and we have never quarrelled. I remember seeing him in the Fleece Tap [a small room at the rear of the main *Fleece Hotel* in Head Street] *one night a few years ago. It was between six and seven in the evening and I was sitting drinking some porter* [dark brown bitter beer] *when he came in and sat down beside me. He later asked me if I remembered old Mr Holt who had been found dead in the river all those years ago. When I said that I did not, he told me that he had been killed at the Blue Pig* [a pub in Head Street] *and that he had been there at the time and had helped another man commit the murder. He told me that Holt had been drinking in the Blue Pig one night in 1788 and that he had later gone outside and sat sleeping on the steps of Mr Smythies' house next door* [currently Woolworth's]. *At about twelve o'clock he said that he and a man named Roger Munsey had gone up to him and that Munsey had hit him over the head with a crow bar and killed him. They then put him in a sack and hid him in the cellar of the Blue Pig* [the cellar door apparently led directly onto the street]. *They then got some sawdust to cover the blood on the ground and tried to wash away the blood which had spilled onto the steps. He never told me what became of the body after that, but we were both sober at the time of the conversation.*

Head Street, looking towards North Hill, c. 1890. The Blue Pig *public house would have been somewhere opposite the tall building seen about half way along on the left side of the street which until recently was the town's main post office, and is now converted into a multiplex cinema.* Jess Jephcott

And that was really the extent of the case for the prosecution. An alleged confession that was made some three years previously and then never spoken of again. It was going to be difficult to secure a conviction without further evidence. Lester had apparently been sworn to secrecy by Williams and had managed to keep details of the conversation to himself for several weeks afterwards. When further questioned by the court he said that after about three or four weeks he had decided to tell his wife about the conversation, and that he had also spoken of the matter with Mr Hill, the landlord of the *Fleece Tap*. Apparently, the matter had been playing on his mind and he had been having difficulty in sleeping at nights. He said that this all took place about three years ago and that he had never spoken of it again since being brought before Mr Abel, one of the Justices at Colchester, a few weeks previously. Apparently, the rumour mill had been working overtime with details of the prisoner's supposed involvement in the murder being spoken of in all the bars and taverns of the town. At length, the prisoner decided to make an official complaint to the Town Clerk's Office, stating that his character had been scandalised about the town by Lester, and requested that a summons be brought against him in order that he might clear his name. When questioned, Lester explained that he had not

Culver Street looking towards the junction with Head Street, c.1930. The large building on the left is the Fleece Hotel *which fronted on to Head Street. The tap bar, or public bar, was at the rear of the building accessed from Culver Street.*
Author's collection

been responsible for spreading any rumours about Charles Williams, and adding that he would never have mentioned anything about what Williams had said to him had it not been for the situation that he currently found himself in, and being questioned by the justices. Of course, Lester could well have been speaking the truth. The rumours of William's confession to the crime could have been stirred up, or perpetuated, by Lester's wife, or even the landlord of the *Fleece Tap* whom Lester had also taken into his confidence. It is also possible that Williams himself had made more than one confession of his guilt to others whom he had met during his various travels.

Another difficulty facing the court was the fact that there was scarcely anyone left alive who had been connected with the original case. The coroner, the jury, the surgeons who had examined the body, were all dead. Only one person was left alive who had been involved with the case and who had seen Mr Holt's body after it had been retrieved from the river. This was sixty-four-year-old Esau Ladbrook who had known Daniel Holt when he lived at Lexden. When called to the stand for the prosecution he recounted his version of events as he remembered it:

> I saw Mr Holt's body when he was dead – it was lying in an outhouse near the River Colne at Rowhedge. After the doctor had removed the skin from his head I saw two bloody specks on the skull-bone, on the left side. There were no marks on his face – no sign of any damage caused by crabs or things of that sort. I could see no cut or stab on any part of his body and the doctors said that there were no fractures to the head.

During cross-examination, Mr Ladbrook confirmed that these events had indeed taken place thirty-five years ago and that the place where the body had been found was some three miles from the *Blue Pig*. He also made the point that even if the body had been thrown into the river at Colchester, it could easily have floated down to Donyland if the tide was set that way.

Among the other witnesses called was Elizabeth Buckingham who said that her mother and father used to keep the *Blue Pig* public house in 1788. She said that she

St Peter's church on North Hill, looking towards the junction with High Street and Head Street. At the foot of the hill the road passes over the River Colne and North Bridge. Author's collection

remembered seeing Mr Holt in her father's house about three days before he went missing. She said that he was in the company of two bad women, but that she never saw him leave. Another witness who was called, this time on behalf of the defence, was John Verlander who claimed to be the son of the person who kept the *Blue Pig* in 1788 (possibly the brother of the last witness), and who gave the following testimony:

> *I recollect Mr Holt being there on the night in question, in the company of two women of loose character. They stayed there until about ten o'clock and then left the house together. They turned in the opposite direction from Mr Smythies' steps and went in the direction of the river. I also knew the prisoner Williams and am quite sure that he was not at the Pig on that evening. The cellar door was always kept shut at night and secured by an iron grating. I am quite certain that the body of the deceased man could not have been brought into the Pig concealed in a sack, or in any other manner, or else I would have known about it. I never saw or heard of any blood or sawdust on the steps, which was well used by the public, or elsewhere. I must have seen it had there been any.*

After hearing the evidence of just one more witness, the Judge intervened in the proceedings and directing his comments towards the Jury explained that from the nature of the case proved thus far by the witnesses, it would be quite impossible to convict the prisoner. In the first place it would be necessary to prove that the deceased had actually been murdered. And secondly, if the surgeons who examined the body all those years ago could find no evidence of foul play, resulting in the coroner's jury returning a verdict of Accidental Death, how could this court, held thirty-five years after the event, prove otherwise and convict the prisoner of the charge?

Summing up, his Lordship stated that the circumstances surrounding the prisoner's alleged confession were indeed rather strange and that he could think of no reason for his having acting in this manner. It was not, for example, a confession made in the heat of the moment, or occasioned by a sudden expression of guilt, but rather coolly to one of his companions over a pint of porter, and at such a distance of time after the event. He therefore directed the Jury to return a verdict of Not Guilty and Charles Williams was released from custody. What really happened to Daniel Holt on that cold January evening will perhaps never be known.

The River Colne at North Bridge in 1880 where Daniel Holt's body may have been disposed of. The riverside path seen to the right of the picture is still a popular route between North Station Road and Castle Park. Horatio Hunnable

CHAPTER 3

Highway Robbery at Manwood Hill
1789

*She was found about forty-five minutes later lying
unconscious in a pool of blood.*

The area known locally as 'Manwood Hill' is situated midway between Colchester and the villages of Abberton and Langenhoe, on the road to Mersea Island. In distance, it is perhaps little more than a mile or so from the outskirts of Colchester, but is, nevertheless, an area of open countryside and woodland. In fact, the area bordering the main highway is heavily wooded on both sides of the road and certainly not the kind of place that one would want to be found wandering and isolated on a dark evening. This would particularly have been the case in the late eighteenth century when assaults against travellers were still a common crime.

This period was also, of course, still very much the heyday of the mounted highwayman, or footpad, criminals who made their living by preying on vulnerable travellers along quiet roads and country lanes. They would usually operate in areas where there was plenty of cover for them to hide and would prefer situations where their 'prey' would be at a disadvantage – such as on steep hills, or perhaps along poorly made up roads where they might be travelling slowly - making them tempting targets. And, of course, the rewards for the would-be robber could be substantial, for with few banks around and no credit cards or cheques, many people carried their money and valuables around with them. From a modern perspective, the myth of the highwayman still conjures up images of a 'Robin Hood' type figure, whose aim in life was to rob the rich to help the poor, but in reality, of course, these men were vicious outlaws who had little pity or concern for their helpless victims.

The incident which we are now going to examine has all the hallmarks of a case of highway robbery, and indeed probably did begin with that objective in mind. But in this case the

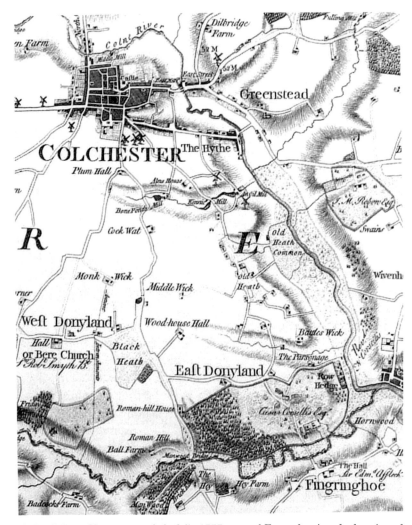

A detail from Chapman and André's 1777 map of Essex showing the location of Manwood at the southern-most tip of the page. Peter Evans

victims of the crime decided to put up a fight, with devastating consequences. The attack took place on the evening of Saturday, 24 October 1789 when Mr and Mrs Samuel Deeks of Abberton, and Mr Sheppard Stammers of Peldon, were returning home from Colchester market on horseback at about seven o'clock. As they were making their way up Manwood Hill towards the village of Langenhoe they were attacked by three footpads who immediately demanded that they hand over their money. Mr Deeks' first reaction was to call upon his friend, Mr Stammers to 'Knock him down.', which he immediately did. However, another one of the gang rushed forwards towards Mr Deeks and presented a large horse pistol to his head with menacing intent. Realising that the situation was hopeless, Mr Deeks immediately submitted and taking out his money said, 'Here friend, take all my money, but don't use it ill.' The villain, without a word of reply, then knocked the money from his hand and discharged his pistol in the direction of Mr Deek's head. The ball passed close to his face leaving burn marks on his cheek and throat, before passing through his shoulder and lodging in his wife's head (she had been sitting behind him on the same horse, and had unfortunately stooped for shelter at the wrong moment). Mrs Deeks instantly fell to the ground whilst the startled horse set off at a gallop towards the interior of the wood, with her injured husband still in the saddle.

Having been rendered almost senseless and faint by the loss of blood, the poor man eventually fell from his horse and lay on the ground for some considerable time before coming to and regaining his senses. At length he managed to crawl his way out of the wood and, with some difficulty, managed to make his way to a cottage where he was able to send someone to look for his wife. She was found about forty-five minutes later lying unconscious in a pool of blood. She was taken at once to the house of a friend who immediately summoned medical assistance.

The surgeons who attended her, upon probing the wound, found that the ball from the pistol had entered through her right ear and had lodged about two inches inside her head, in a part so well supplied with blood vessels that any attempt to remove it would have been fraught with danger. Amazingly, she was still alive at this point and was perfectly conscious when examined by the surgeons, although the prognosis was poor and she was not expected to live for very long. As for her husband, his condition was also the cause of great concern and it was expected that the wounds of both of them would prove fatal.

In the days which followed the incident a number of individuals were apprehended on suspicion of having been involved in the crime, but due to lack of evidence were all discharged. It had been noted by several residents that a trio of rather unsavoury looking characters had been seen begging in the district for two or three days prior to the crime and there was good reason for believing that they were somehow involved. But with no regular police force to hunt and track them down the scent quickly went cold. One must remember, of course, that the only form of policing, or crime detection, in those days was that which was provided by the parish constable, who was often an unpaid volunteer taking a year off from his day job. In fact, according to one contemporary report of the period, the typical parish constable was a person who vanished just as quickly as the smoke from his pipe at the first sign of trouble. Such comments, of course, were perhaps a little unfair as the majority of them were just ordinary citizens who had received little or no training for the job in hand, and who had more than likely been pressed into service in the first place.

In fact, such were the general concerns about rising crime

Market day in Colchester High Street in the 1850s. Despite the street being full of people and animals, a few horse-drawn vehicles can be seen making their way through the crowds.

Author's collection

figures in the late eighteenth century, and with little or no attempts initiated by government to solve the problem, many members of the public, particularly those from the wealthier sections of the community who had more to lose, joined one of the many Associations which were being set up throughout the country for the aim of bringing criminals to justice. They were properly known as 'Associations for the Prosecution of Felons' and would provide their members with financial assistance in bringing those responsible for committing crimes to the courts to be prosecuted. Surprisingly, at this period in our judicial system, there was no such thing as a public prosecutor's office where some local or government official could be relied upon to investigate a crime and prosecute those responsible. This task was left to the victim of the crime who, at their own expense, had to initiate court proceedings and then act as prosecutor in court.

In order, therefore, to provide some form of assistance for their members who had suffered some form of criminal injustice, the Associations would provide financial help in the form of offering reward money for information leading to the arrest and conviction of the party concerned. They often also employed their own 'constable' or 'thief-catcher' (today's private detectives) and would usually assist in the cost of prosecuting the case in court. Each new member of an Association would have to pay an initial signing-on fee of perhaps a guinea or so, depending on their ability to pay, and then an annual subscription of something in the order of five or ten shillings. The value of the rewards offered would usually be linked to the type of crime committed, and could range in value from about ten shillings for stealing some eggs, to £20 or more for murder, rape, arson or highway robbery.

Fortunately, Mr Deeks appears to have been a member of the 'Winstree Hundred Association for the Prosecution of Felons' and the group were quick to offer a reward for information leading to the arrest of the individuals concerned. In fact, the advertisement, which appeared in the *Ipswich Journal* on Saturday, 31 October 1789 (and which is reproduced below) just seven days after the event, seems to have been posted by a close member of Mr Deeks family –

certainly someone with the same name as the victim. Could this perhaps have been his father, or even his son. It is also possible, of course, that the poor man posted the reward himself whilst lying on his own deathbed, as the wording of the advertisement suggests that the victim's injuries were so severe as to likely prove fatal.

ROBBERY

Whereas on Saturday last, the 24th of October instant, in Man-wood, in the parish of Langenhoe in Essex, about seven o'clock in the evening Mr Sheppard Stammers of Peldon, and Mr Samuel Deeks of Abberton, and his Wife, being on horseback on their way home from Colchester market, were stopped by three footpads; who demanded their money, when one of them, without waiting to receive the money which Mr Deeks held in his hand, and offered them, discharged a pistol at Mr and Mrs Deeks, whereby it is feared they are both mortally wounded.

Whoever will give information of the person who actually fired the said pistol (although an accomplice) shall, upon his conviction receive a reward of FIFTY POUNDS over and above the reward offered by act of parliament, and over and above the reward of FIVE POUNDS already offered by the Winstree Hundred Association, to be paid by me,

SAMUEL DEEKS.

N.B. Two of the above footpads appeared to be about five feet eight or nine inches high, the other about five feet five, one of the tallest had on a surtout light-coloured great coat, the other two had on short jackets, the one brown the other blue, and all round hats.

It is interesting to note that the value of the reward money offered amounted to at least £55 (worth about £4,000 today), not including an unspecified sum that would have been payable from the government. Further expense, of course, would have been required to take the case to court in the event that the culprits had been apprehended, making the whole business of crime detection and prosecution a costly affair. This is one reason, no doubt, why so many crimes of the period went undetected, and also why the authorities adopted a policy of inflicting severe punishments on those people who were caught, in the belief that it would act as a deterrent to others. For example, at the beginning of the nineteenth century there were more than 200 crimes on the so called 'Bloody Code', that is crimes which carried the death penalty. By way of illustration, some of the more trivial types of crime for which a person could be sent to the gallows included pick-pocketing, shop-lifting, stealing a letter or associating for more than a month with gypsies.

But to return to the case in question and, in particular, to the fate of Mr and Mrs Deeks. The wound to Mrs Deeks apparently proved to be fatal, although no mention is made of the fate of her husband. In fact, it has been difficult to discover any information about the couple other than what has already been mentioned. They were described at the time as being 'A very worthy happy couple who had been married but a few months and were greatly esteemed', but as to where they lived, where they got married or even where they were buried remains something of a mystery. As far as the perpetrators of the crime were concerned, it would seem as if they succeeded in escaping detection as no record of the case has been found coming to trial.

This rather lonely stretch of road marks the site of Manwood Bridge where the Colchester - Mersea road crosses over the Roman river. 2004. The Author

CHAPTER 4

The Murder of Thomas Patrick
1827

*...the two men started to fight each other and...
were rolling around in the gutter...*

*The sentence of the court is that you, Reuben Martin, be taken
to the place from whence you came, and on Monday next, to
the place of execution, there to be hanged by the neck until you
are dead, and that your body be given to the surgeons for
dissection, according to the directions of the statute; and may
the Lord have mercy on your soul....Amen.*

Such were the words spoken to Reuben Martin (alias James Winters and Big Jem) as he stood in the dock at the *Nisi Prius* court (a special court convened by agreement and presided over by a single judge and jury) convened at Chelmsford Shire Hall on Saturday, 8 December 1827. His crime had been the brutal slaying of a Colchester publican just two weeks earlier and now he was about to suffer the penalty prescribed by law – execution by hanging.

The crime had taken place in the Magdalen Street area of Colchester in the early hours of Sunday, 25 November 1827. This particular district was one of the poorer, and more socially deprived parts of the town which contained a profusion of public houses (in Magdalen Street alone there were at least fourteen – the equivalent of one pub for every forty-two yards!), most of which served as a catalyst for riotous or drunken behaviour, particularly at weekends. One of these pubs was the *Yorkshire Grey* which stood on the south side of Magdalen Street, not far from the junction with Wimpole Road, and from where the disastrous events of this particular evening were to unfold. The landlord of the pub was forty-five-year-old Thomas Patrick, a well respected man in the community and a local churchwarden. On the evening of 24 November 1827 Patrick had arranged for a sale of clothing (by order of the parish overseer) which had belonged to a recently deceased parishioner in the bar of his public house. By all accounts the sale had attracted a goodly crowd which had included a local man named Isaac Parsons, a bone-gatherer, together with his common-law wife. During the evening Parsons had purchased a great-coat from the deceased man's belongings and at about half past eleven he and his wife had decided to make their way home. They left the pub with his wife carrying the coat over her arm and proceeded to make their way along the road in the direction of Water Lane (now Brook Street). For some reason Isaac's attention was momentarily diverted and he allowed his wife to walk on ahead. Within seconds the accused (Big Jem), who was accompanied by two men named George Johnson and George Osborne, came up to her and said, 'My dear, what have we got here?'. Her husband quickly came running up and asked him what he was doing and told his wife to go on ahead. What followed was the beginning of a disastrous sequence of events which was to result in the death of the landlord Thomas Patrick and the arrest of Big Jem for his murder.

Although instigated entirely by Big Jem, the two men started to fight each other and before long both were rolling around in the gutter as a small group of onlookers gathered to watch. At length Big Jem managed to get the upper hand and proceeded to rifle through the helpless man's pockets looking for money and a watch which he thought his victim was concealing. By this time Mr Patrick, the landlord, had been alerted to the commotion and had decided that it would be best to go and get help from Jeremiah Boyles, the local constable. When Boyles arrived he immediately caught hold of Big Jem while at the same time instructing Mr Patrick and another man named John Crooks to assist him. At this point the assailant struggled and struck Boyles a tremendous blow to the face which knocked him senseless. The prisoner then made his escape whilst Crooks and Patrick struggled to take his accomplices, Johnson and Osborne into custody.

Within a fairly short space of time Big Jem had armed himself with a stout piece of wooden fencing to use as a weapon, and at least two other police constables had joined in the struggle to apprehend him. He was clearly in a mood to do serious harm to someone and the situation was rapidly getting out of hand. Armed with this menacing piece of wood, which he had ripped from some nearby garden fencing, Big Jem prepared himself to attack his pursuers. Unfortunately for Mr Patrick he was to be the first in line. During the struggle to arrest and imprison Johnson and Osborne, Patrick had broken off to secure the help of yet another constable (Cant) and was walking along the road towards his house, when he was confronted by the accused who, with both arms raised, brought the piece of wood thundering down onto his head. Patrick fell to the ground, instantly dead, with blood gushing from his wound. This brutal attack on an unarmed man was seen by several witnesses including one Isaac Hawkins, a paviour, who lived in Magdalen Street between the *Yorkshire Grey* and *Red Cross* public houses:

> *I was awoken by a noise in the street early on the Sunday morning and got out of bed to have a look out of the window. I saw a group of people standing under a lamp by the Dead Wall and heard a woman shrieking. One of the people (the accused) then left the group and went down to the Red Lion fence and started pulling the palings down. I then saw him coming across the road and making towards my door – he had two pieces of wood in his hand. I then saw another man (Patrick) coming across the road towards him. The prisoner then stepped off the path to the breast of the road, threw down one piece of wood, and then took hold of the other with both hands and struck the deceased on the head, who then fell to the ground. He hit him so hard that it would have knocked a bullock down. He then went off and hit another man [Watts the constable] but he didn't fall. I then went downstairs and discovered that it was Patrick who had been hit on the head.*

Another man who witnessed the event was David Serjeant, a labourer, who said that he was returning home from the *Yorkshire Grey* public house between twelve and one o'clock on Sunday morning:

I was standing by the Cross-bricks and saw Boyles attempt to take the prisoner into custody, before the prisoner knocked him down and ran away. When I got to near the Red Cross, I saw Patrick going towards Cant's house and the prisoner was standing still on the opposite side of the road. He was standing near the gutter and was holding a piece of board which was broader than one of my hands - about three feet long and an inch thick. Patrick came across the road in a slanting direction and had barely got opposite the prisoner when he held up the board with both his hands and struck him on his forehead as hard as he could. I was no more than five yards away at the time. The prisoner then went off in the direction of the Yorkshire Grey where he also attacked constable Watts with the same piece of wood.

Marianne Crooks also told the court that she had been up on the Sunday morning and had seen the scuffle between the prisoner and Parsons. She said that about half an hour later the prisoner came to her door and asked her to let him look at his hand, which was very bloody, and to knock a nail out of a piece of wood. When she refused to get involved he proceeded to knock the nail out on her doorstep, saying 'he had already served one man out, and that the first b-----y b------r that came across him he would serve him the same.' Whilst the prisoner was at the door of Mrs Crooks, a neighbour of hers on the opposite side of the road, called out that she had been told that poor Mr Patrick had been murdered. The prisoner, who must have heard this, then quickly made his escape from the scene and hid himself in a barn in Maldon Lane (Maldon Road), about a mile distant, where he remained until about eight o'clock the next morning. In fact, the murder weapon was later found in a wagon close to the barn. On the Sunday morning Big Jem continued to make good his escape along the road towards Coggeshall where he was later that same day apprehended by one of the Town Serjeants.

In the early hours of the Sunday morning, the Mayor and Magistrates had been made aware of what had taken place and the Town Serjeants had been active in despatching persons in every direction with a description of the murderer. Some information had been gained that he had taken the London Road, and so it was that Town Serjeants, Harvey and Cant, proceeded towards Coggeshall where they raised the alarm to the residents there. After spending some time searching the district, it was Harvey who finally spotted the prisoner hiding in a wooded area and apprehended him at about twelve o'clock midday.

By about half past three in the afternoon, Harvey and Cant had arrived back in Colchester with the prisoner who was seen to be laughing as he was being led along the road. Several witnesses soon identified him as the person who had committed the crime, but he continued to remain quite indifferent to the seriousness of his situation – that is until he had been heavily shackled, at which time his demeanour began to change and he became more subdued, obviously at last realising what lay ahead of him.

On the next day (Monday, 26 November) he was brought before the Mayor and Magistrates sitting in the Moot Hall, where after a six hour session they returned a verdict of Wilful Murder against him. On Wednesday, 28 November he was again brought before the Magistrates where evidence earlier given to the Coroner's court was read over. When asked if he had anything to say in answer to the charge, the prisoner

The old Moot Hall in Colchester High Street. Dating from the twelfth century, the Moot Hall was the town's centre for administration and justice until its removal in 1843. The present Town Hall, which opened in 1902, stands on the same site.
Author's collection

replied: 'It may all be true for what I know – I know nothing about it – it is a mystery to me.' The prisoner was then formally charged with the murder and on the following evening was sent off to the newly-built prison at Springfield, Chelmsford on the nine o'clock Wellington coach. A large crowd had gathered outside the Moot Hall to witness his departure and the prisoner responded by continually nodding to people in the crowd until he was out of sight.

Such then were the events that brought Big Jem to be standing before the Judge at the Shire Hall, Chelmsford on Saturday, 8 December 1827 to witness his Lordship performing the painful task of pronouncing the sentence of death upon him. Throughout the trial the prisoner had remained standing, listening intently to the numerous witnesses as they gave evidence against him. He appeared to be a man of great muscular strength, standing about five feet seven inches high and having a small head which seemed to be out of proportion to the rest of his body. He had dark hair; a ruddy complexion; a short neck and his face was pitted with scars from smallpox. During the proceedings, to which he had pleaded 'Not Guilty', he reaffirmed that he could remember nothing of the incident and that he was a stranger to that part of the town. After the judge had completed his summarisation

The Shire Hall at Chelmsford where the Essex Quarter Sessions and Assize courts were held. The prisoners who were awaiting trial were held in the basement from where steps led up directly into the court room.
Author's collection

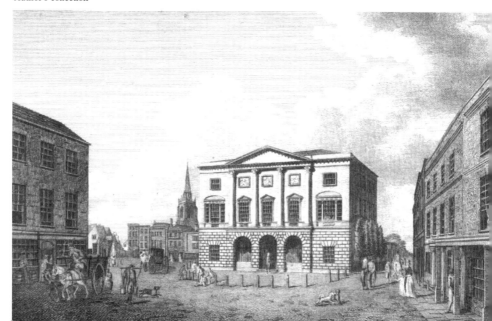

of the proceedings, and just as the case was about to go to the jury, the prisoner cried out in a firm voice, and whilst pointing to his own head, said that there was clear proof that he himself had been wounded on the head (in other words, it was not a totally one-sided affair). The prisoner did indeed have a scar on his head and was also sporting a black eye. He continued to relate that he had drunk about three pints of gin on the night in question and that this had heated his blood somewhat. The prisoner apparently spoke these words with astonishing firmness and conviction which, for a few moments, seemed to create a degree of sympathy for him among those in the court.

The jury, however, took no longer than twenty minutes to return a verdict of 'Guilty of Murder.' As soon as the Judge had finished relaying the details of the sentence upon him, the prisoner appeared to stand rigidly still for several seconds, seemingly wondering whether or not he should say anything, before finally releasing his grasp on the bar in front of him, and sitting down. Once the court had been partially cleared, the gaoler and his assistants proceeded to convey the prisoner towards the vehicle in which he was to be taken 'to the place from whence he came', in accordance with the sentence. When he reached the open space of the Market Place, and to show the crowd that he had not lost his courage, he threw his hat high into the air saying that it was not his own, and that he would carry nothing out of the world but that which belonged to him. He was then taken to the Convict Gaol to await the execution of his sentence in forty-eight hours' time.

When he had finally reached his last abode he became very alerted to his situation and asked if some portions of scripture could be read to him. On the following day his sister (who lived in London) arrived at his request to see him. As she entered the cell he was heard to say: 'You have seen me in a similar situation once before, but I am nearer my death now than I was then.' During the visit, which lasted a full two hours, the occasional tear was seen to fall from his eyes as the two conversed. His sister was described as being handsomely dressed and well mannered, and had apparently only learned of the true extent of her brother's situation after arriving in Chelmsford earlier in the day. She also informed the prison officials that her brother's real name was, in fact, James Winters, and that her family lived near Stevenage in Hertfordshire. Following the visit of his sister the prisoner spent much of his remaining time in the prison chapel in an attempt to come to terms with the dreadful situation in which he now found himself, and is known to have received the sacrament before he suffered.

The place of execution was, for the first time, in front of the new convict prison at Springfield, directly over the entrance and in full view of the crowd. After being led out to the scaffold to meet his fate the prisoner refrained from addressing the crowd – as was the custom – and with the minimum of fuss submitted to his punishment. By this time his mother had also arrived in the town to join his sister, although they had been unable to gain access to the hanging due to the large crowd in attendance. They had even been told by one rather unruly person present (who had failed to realise who they were) that they would not be able to get a place even for the sum of £40. And now as the prisoner was led on to the platform, his body was momentarily in full view of the assembled crowd.

The convict gaol at Springfield, Chelmsford in 1829. Until 1868 all hangings in Britain were carried out in public, and large crowds would often assemble to witness the grisly spectacle. In most cases the platform itself was shielded with wooden boards, with black cloth drapes, to conceal the lower body of the usually struggling prisoner. Author's collection

However, as soon as the trap-door had been released his body fell partially from view, leaving only the upper part visible. His body had fallen sharply, causing the apparatus to move several inches, and his hanging body was seen to convulse for several seconds before becoming limp. After his body was allowed to hang for the prescribed hour (to ensure that death occurred), it was cut down and taken to the prison infirmary for dissection, where it was viewed by many prominent local men.

Following Thomas Patrick's death his wife Elizabeth took over the running of the *Yorkshire Grey* public house. Her husband's body was buried in the nearby churchyard of St Mary Magdalen Church and a headstone placed over the grave which recorded the following epitaph:

> *By Murderous Hands my life was taken away*
> *And here I rest until the Judgement Day*
> *I've left a Wife and Children dear,*
> *To mourn my loss, the stroke it was severe.*

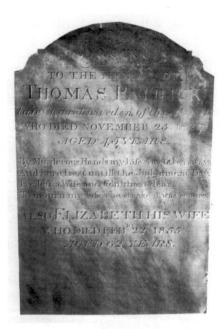

Thomas Patrick's tombstone in St Mary Magdalen churchyard.
Colchester Archaeological Trust

CHAPTER 5

A Tale of Murder at Wix
c.1840

...ghostly happenings.... at Red House Farm.

A few years ago one of the churchwardens of the parish of Wix in Essex, discovered an interesting collection of old papers in the parish chest. Among them was an intriguing account of a murder and ghostly happenings which had apparently taken place in the parish in the 1830s or 40s, at a place called Red House Farm. The account was in the handwriting of the Reverend Proctor Benwell (Vicar of Wix 1883-1908) and concerned a story which had been told to him several years earlier by a man named John Vincent Riff, a former resident of Red House Farm. It is not clear how long after having heard the tale that the Reverend Benwell decided to write it down, but it purports to be an accurate account of what he was told. The original account is entitled 'Auditory Local Phantasm at Wickes, Essex' and a full transcript of the account, albeit with minor alterations, is given below:

In the year 1868 or 1869 when I was 28 or 29 years of age I was living at Red House Farm in the parish of Wickes, about 14 miles from Colchester, and eight miles from Harwich. The house is at the extreme east end of the parish bordering on the parish of Great Oakley. It was the last in the village on the left hand side of the high road coming from Colchester. It stands back some yards from the road and is approached by two entrances to the front and side doors respectively. From the back kitchen a door opened into a yard. Within the house these doors communicated with three passages.

One evening about the end of November I was alone in the house. All the doors were locked. I had been sitting reading for an hour or two before the dining room fire. When about nine o'clock I heard footsteps coming along the stone passage that led from the kitchen and the cat, which was sitting at my feet

The main Harwich to Colchester Road as it passes through the village of Wix.
c.1906. John Norman

in front of the fender, rushed under the table with all his hairs on end. The steps came as far as the door which opened from the dining room into this passage and seemed to stop there. I could not make it out and listened intently for about 10 minutes after which time the footsteps went about half way up the staircase leading up from the passage just outside the door and then they suddenly stopped and I heard no more. I caught up my poker and ran up the stairs into my bedroom and, taking down my sword, searched every bedroom but found no one. I then went downstairs and tried all the doors and I also found that all the lower windows were fastened and that no one could have got into or out of the house.

The next day as I was working in the garden the owner of the house Mr Maurice Constable of White House rode up, and after asking me how I was said 'Did you hear anything last night?'. I told him what I had heard and he said 'This is the very night, John, that my father was murdered.'

Then he told me that one Saturday night his father had come back from Colchester market and while he was having tea with his wife in the same dining room, there came a knock at the side door and the servant came in and said that a beggar man wanted bread and cheese and a place to sleep. The old people told her to find him supper and a bed in the room over the back kitchen, which was entered by the stairs from the kitchen.

About nine o'clock when the old lady had gone to bed and the old gentleman was counting his money and looking over his accounts this tramp walked along the passage from the kitchen (he wore hobnailed boots) and looking, it is presumed, through the glass panel, which was in the door, and seeing how his host was engaged he entered the room and after a scuffle murdered the old man. He went out by the same door and was going up the stairs but evidently the old lady had heard a noise and had come out of her room, she looked over the staircase and seeing it was this tramp coming up, she threw down a bushel skip (a heavy corn measure with iron bands) and killed him. She was tried for manslaughter and acquitted.

Mr Constable further said that he had not told me this before because there had been difficulty in letting the house as it was looked on as being haunted. I had not previously heard that it bore that reputation.

The next year, on the same day of the month, I was sitting in the dining room when everything occurred in the same way as before except that the cat was not present. I was not expecting it, and had forgotten all about it. This time I set it

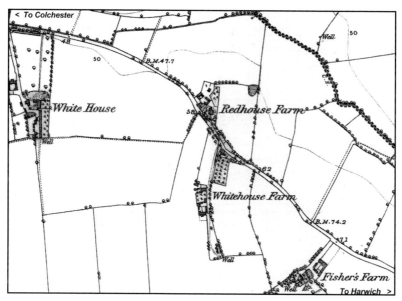

Detail from a late nineteenth century Ordnance Survey map showing the location of Redhouse Farm. Author's collection

down to something ghostly and did not stir but went on
reading. I was alone in the house and all the doors and
windows were fastened as on the former occasion. Before the
next anniversary I had left the house.

It is indeed a remarkable story, and one that appears to have a
ring of truth about it. For example, the details regarding the
location of the house, and the name of the former owner, are
all correct. However, all attempts to authenticate this tale
through documentary evidence have proved futile. There does
not appear to be any record of a court case involving a Mrs
Constable having killed anyone, or even that of her husband
having been murdered. Neither has there been found any
report relating to such a crime in the local press, which surely
must have been reported at the time.

If anything, what little evidence that has surfaced relating to
the account would appear to pour scorn on the whole saga.
For instance, John Maurice Constable, the 'old gentleman',
and father of the said Maurice Constable, who was supposedly
murdered by the tramp, actually died at the relatively young
age of forty-two. Interestingly, however, his death was sudden
and unexpected, but his obituary notice in the Essex Standard
for 11 August 1832 simply states that he died 'after only two
days of illness.' His death is further recorded on a memorial
tablet on the north wall of Wix parish church, which reads as
follows:

> *Death seized upon him unexpectedly*
> *in the flower of his age; leaving to us*
> *who survive a melancholy example*
> *of the uncertainty of human life and*
> *admonishing all men to remember*
> *the words of the Lord Jesus.*
> *"Take ye heed, watch and pray,*
> *for ye know not when the time is."*

It is true, of course, that the wording does suggest an unusual
death, but there is nothing to add credence to the notion that
he was murdered.

And there is always the possibility, of course, that in the

process of the story being repeated and recalled, that the John Maurice Constable referred to by Mr Maurice Constable as having been his father, was in fact his grandfather, who coincidentally had the same name. This would also fit in better with the occupant of the house being described in the story as an 'old gentleman'. But even this theory fails to stand up to scrutiny because his grandfather's death certificate clearly states that he died peacefully of 'old age' (aged seventy-eight) in 1843.

Whatever the truth of the affair, it certainly makes for an interesting tale, and one where the truth of the matter may eventually be revealed.

CHAPTER 6

Who Killed John Harding?
1870

*… a labourer … had found the boy's body whilst
digging sand from the pit…*

The suspicious death of fourteen-year-old John Harding of Colchester in April 1870 caused great excitement in the town as rumours spread that he had been killed by his parents. The story goes that having misbehaved in some small way he had been frightened to go home and had spent the best part of a week roaming the streets and getting his meals the best way that he could. At length his parents managed to catch up with him and gave him such a hiding that the poor lad died. The panic-stricken parents then put his body into a coal sack and took him to a nearby sandpit where they buried him. Of course, this was all supposition and rumour – there being no firm evidence that the parents had done any such thing - but the boy had indeed suffered a nasty

Colchester Infantry Camp, c.1865. Note that members of the public appear to be freely mixing with the troops, something which would not be allowed to happen today. Author's collection

injury to the side of his head and his body had been found buried in the sandpit.

The Harding family lived in a small house in Proud's Yard, Military Road, not far from the large army camp. The accommodation must have been quite sparse for the entire family, including both parents and five children, all slept in one room. The children of the family were John aged fourteen (the deceased): James, ten; William, seven; Samuel, five; and a younger daughter whose name is not recorded. Their father, George Harding, an army pensioner, and their mother, Johanna Griffin Harding, earned their living by running a small greengrocery shop from their home. Mrs Harding also used to travel round the area hawking vegetables from a donkey and cart.

It would seem that 'Johnny' had run off from home on Thursday, 21 April 1870, some time between twelve and one o'clock in the afternoon, and after spending the next five days dodging his parents, had finally met his death sometime during the early hours of the following Tuesday morning. The timing was deduced from the fact that when his body was discovered on the afternoon of Tuesday 26, April, medical experts were of the opinion that it had been lying there for nearly twelve hours.

Military Road, looking north towards the town centre, in the 1930s. The large building on the opposite side of the road is Camp Church which was built at the time of the Crimean War to support the nearby infantry barracks. Author's collection

The police and a medical officer were called to examine the corpse before it was removed to the nearby *Mermaid* beerhouse on Mersea Road. It was from here that the inquest into the cause of death was opened the following afternoon, an inquiry that was to last for two weeks and involve the appearance of no less than sixteen witnesses called to give evidence.

At the commencement of the Inquiry the Coroner, Mr Adolphus Church, explained to the Jury the nature of the case before them and said that their first duty would be to view the body before proceeding to the spot where it was found. After that he suggested that it might be more convenient for all concerned, including members of the public, if they then adjourned to the Magistrates' Room at the Town Hall. After completing this necessary business the court reconvened and the Coroner called for the first witness. This was Elijah Dessent, a labourer in the employ of Mr Jones (solicitor), who had found the boy's body whilst digging sand from the pit on the afternoon in question:

> *On Tuesday afternoon, about two o'clock, I went to the sandpit, along with the boy Dyer, who is carting sand to West Bergholt. I went into the pit and began to dig and I found that the sand was very loose. After I had moved about a shovel full of sand I came upon the arm of a body. It was about six inches below the surface and I got hold of it and felt along until I got to the elbow and discovered that it was someone dead lying there. My companion, Walter Sparkes, who was with me in the pit at the time, had to get out then because he couldn't bear it. We then both went to the house of Mr Beach (owner of adjacent house) who then returned to the pit with us. After that I cleared away some more sand and exposed the head. Mr Beach's man, Alfred Chambers, then took hold of his arm with me and we pulled him out. The body was doubled up and lying on its right side, with the left arm being curled up.*

The CORONER: *Did you notice any bruises?*
Answer: *On the breast I saw some.*
The FOREMAN: *But didn't he have his clothes on?*
Answer: *Yes he had, but his breast was naked.*

The CORONER: *Can you describe his appearance more fully?*
Answer: *He was wearing a blue jacket and black trousers and his head was lying on his cap, which was beneath his head. There was also some bruising on the right side of his face.*

The court then heard evidence from Mr E Waylen, surgeon, who had been summoned to see the body shortly after it had been found. He said that he thought that the body had been lying in the pit for between ten and twelve hours and that there was a large bruise on the right side of the face which extended from the eye to the chin. When the body had been moved to the *Mermaid* beerhouse he unbuttoned the waistcoat and made a further examination.

The CORONER: *Can you explain how the bruising to the side of the face might have occurred?*
Answer: *The bruise might have been done by a fist or a fall, but certainly not by a stick.*

He then described to the court the results of the post-mortem examination which he had conducted earlier in the day and

A late Victorian view of the High Street, looking east, with the gothic spire of St Nicholas's church clearly visible. High Street was the main through road for traffic passing between London and the east coast. Jess Jephcott

concluded by saying that although he could not give a firm opinion as to the exact cause of death, the boy did appear to have suffered from a weak constitution and that any slight shock to the system, or indeed a blow to the body, might have caused his death. He added, however, that the child must have been dead before the sand was covered over him.

A JUROR: *Do you think that the injury to the side of the face could have been the cause of death?*
Answer: *In my opinion the blow to the side of the face would have been sufficient to cause syncope (loss of consciousness or fainting) and consequently death. If there was a blow it must have been from a flat instrument of some kind.*

Another witness called to give evidence at this time was Henry Branch, a farmer residing on Mersea Road close to where the body was found. He told the court that on the afternoon in question he had been alerted to the fact that a body had been found in the sandpit by his son. He then went out to the pit and while he was there said that he saw the deceased's father, George Harding, turn up:

> *While I was standing there looking on his father came up and said to a Sergeant who was standing there, 'What do you think of this? He's murdered, and I am threatened, and I expect that I shall be the next, but I intend to take a good stick with me to give the return blow.' That is all I heard, and all I know about.*

The hearing was then adjourned until the following Wednesday evening. During the ensuing week the town was abuzz with excitement as the inhabitants eagerly awaited any news as to how the police enquiries were proceeding. Many were of the opinion that the boy's parents were somehow involved and so when the Inquiry reconvened it was no surprise that the courtroom was densely crowded. And the fact that the deceased's mother and two of his younger brothers were due to give evidence, only added to their excitement.

After hearing the evidence of William Good, landlord of the *Britannia* public house in Berechurch Road, who told the court that the deceased had come to his bar to ask the time at half past nine on the evening of Monday, 25 April, a hush fell over the court as James Harding, the ten-year-old brother of the deceased made an appearance. After confirming his name and address the Coroner put a series of questions to him that were to last for the next two hours. The following is a shortened version of that examination:

The CORONER: *Did your father ever used to beat Johnny?*
Answer: *No, Sir.*
Question: *What made him keep away from home from the Thursday?*
Answer: *Father came home on Thursday and Johnny, who had forgotten to bring the broom in from the garden, went away somewhere.*
Question: *Why did your brother leave?*
Answer: *I don't know, Sir.*
Question: *Now, little boy, recollect this. Your brother had forgotten*

This drawing of 1870 shows the impressive façade of the Victorian Town Hall. The building was erected in the 1840s and was the centre of local administration and justice until its removal in the late 1890s. Author's collection

the broom. Did your father check him for that?

Answer: *No. Mother said 'Where is the broom! He said, 'I forgot it.'*

Question: *When your brother forgot the broom did your mother check him for it?*

Answer: *No, Sir. Mother told him to fetch it and he went out into the garden and went away.*

Question: *Do you know where Johnny went?*

Answer: *No, Sir. I saw him leave the house and he said he was going after the broom.*

The witness then went on to relate how he had seen his brother on a number of occasions during the week roaming around the army camp:

The CORONER: *Did you ever come near to him?*

Answer: *No. I was never nearer than the length of this hall* [about 12 yards].

Question: *Did you see him on the Sunday?*

Answer: *Yes, I saw him in the Camp.*

Question: *Whom was he with?*

Answer: *The boy Craig. I tried to coax him home, and got him as far as Golden Noble Hill, but he was afraid to go further*[sensation in court].

Question: *What did your brother say?*

Answer: *Johnny asked me if father was at home! I told him he had gone to church, and then, seeing father coming home, Johnny ran away.*

Question: *Did his mother come out?*

Answer: *He ran up the hill, and I caught hold of him. Then mother told me to let him go, and I did not see him after that.*

Question: *Did your mother tell you that someone had said that your brother was killed with a broomstick?*

Answer: *No, Sammy did. A boy named Goody gave him a ha'penny to tell the Militia that mother had killed him.*

Question: *Does your mother know that Sammy said he was killed with a broom?*

Answer: *No, he said with a poker*[sensation]. *Mother told me that Sammy and Bill Goody were up at the fair on the Mersea Road near* *the gravel pit, and that two girls had come into the shop and told her that Sammy was telling a lot of soldiers that she had killed Johnny.*

Question: *What did your mother say?*

Answer: *No one ------I forget.*

Question: *Take time, my boy, and think of your answer.*

Answer: *Mother said, 'No one would understand what the little fellow would say.' She said that Sammy was telling some stories.*

Question: *Did Sammy say anything about Johnny being taken away in a sack?*

Answer: *No. A boy told me that another boy said that mother killed Johnny with a poker, and father took him away in a sack* [sensation].

Towards the close of his evidence the young witness put his hands to his head and fell fainting to the ground. He was at once carried into the Petty Jury room where he was revived. This must have been a tremendous ordeal for the young boy to have gone through, but the Coroner then called for his younger

Military Road, looking south east towards Old Heath and Rowhedge, 2005. The army barracks, which dates from the time of the Crimean War, is located on the right of the road at the top of the hill. The road leading off to the right of the Twist public house is Golden Noble Hill which would have led to the sand pit where the body of John Harding was discovered. Proud's Yard, where the Harding family lived, was a little further down the hill on the same side as the Twist. The Author

brother William, (aged seven), to be questioned. After first trying to impress upon the young lad the nature of an oath, he told the Jury that he would leave it up to them as to what reliance should be placed on his evidence.

The Coroner then proceeded to ask the boy a series of questions which were answered in little more than a whisper, and mostly with just a nod or shake of his head. In particular, the Coroner was trying to ascertain whether his father or mother had been absent from their home at any time during the night before the body was found, and whether or not he had seen his father or mother beating his older brother. However, although he appeared to implicate his parents to some degree, his evidence was full of inconsistencies and it was the general feeling of the Court that it would be quite useless to put any further questions to him. And for the same reasons it was decided not to call his younger brother Samuel (aged five) to give evidence.

The courtroom then fell silent as the dead boy's mother was called and placed in the witness-box. After having been sworn in the Coroner said to her:

> *Before I ask you any questions I may state that, as you already know, there are certain rumours in this case affecting both yourself and your husband. I therefore deem it my duty to tell you that you need not answer any questions tending to incriminate yourself, nor need you make any statement at all unless you like. With that caution, if you would like to make any statement I shall take it down in writing and it will form part of the records of the court and can be used in evidence in any trial. Do you wish to make any statement?*

WITNESS: *Do you mean as to my son that was murdered?*
The CORONER: *Do you wish to make any statement as to this case?*
WITNESS: *Of course I do, why wouldn't I?*
The CORONER: *Then state slowly what you have to say.*

The witness then proceeded to make a rather long and drawn

out statement, part of which is reproduced below:

My son Johnny went away from home on Thursday, 21 April. He was frequently going away, but he had no occasion to do so, only when boys enticed him, and that I could not help, of course. He left my house between twelve and one on Thursday week last, for the purpose of driving the donkey up the garden and putting him into the stable. I told him at the same time to take the broom up and clean out the cart, and to be sure to come back soon, as his father was coming out of hospital at the same time. He came back without the broom and got as far as the door and said, 'Mother, that boy Nelson has made a mess on the floor as usual; I forgot the broom and I'll go back for it.' And I saw no more of him until Sunday afternoon.

I searched for him in different places where the boys told me he was, but could not find him. My son James came to me on Sunday afternoon and said that he had seen his brother up near the Camp Church and that he had coaxed him down as far as Golden Noble Hill. I said, 'Is he on Golden Noble Hill now?' and he replied, 'Yes mother.' So I took my shawl and went there. I told Jemmy [James] to go on before me, and if he could catch him to hold him till I got up. Jemmy caught him just opposite the door of Mr Nevard, who was standing there and looking on all the time. He swung himself out of little Jemmy's hands, and Jemmy not being able to hold him, he [the deceased] then went up Golden Noble Hill again.

Mrs Harding continued:

We did not hear any more of him that day, and on Monday – I am in the habit of going round the Camp with vegetables from half past eight in the morning till twelve or one – as I was going across the big field as usual there was a machine at work on Mr Tettrell's farm and I noticed a person with a blue jacket at the top of the rick, and I thought it was Jack [Johnny]. I said to Jemmy, 'Is that your brother Jack at work on that rick; if he's at work with those men he'll be hungry, and you had better take him some bread (I had some in my cart), and go across the field to him. Jemmy said, 'No mother, Mr Tettrell would put me in prison if I went across the place.', so we then

*came home through the Camp, and my husband emptied the
cart. I told my husband that I thought that I had seen Jack,
and I said I would drive to Mr Tettrell's to see if it was him.
So I went to Mr Tettrell's and found that it was not Jack.*

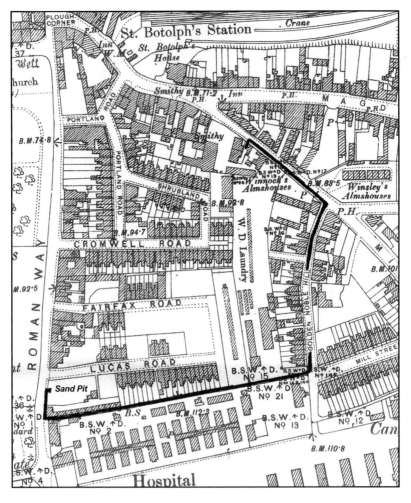

*Part of a nineteenth century Ordnance Survey map showing the location of the sand
pit where John Harding's body was found and Proud's Yard.* Author's collection

Mrs Harding went on to explain that she had spent most of the day out looking for her son before returning home at ten o'clock:

> *When I got home at ten o'clock my husband told me that I had been searching for the boy all day, and that I should not search for him any more that night. He then fastened the door and we went to bed. We never heard any more of him till the man came to the door and said he was covered up in the sand. The door was never opened from the time that it was fastened till the morning, and it was half past eight before I left the house. I am as innocent as a child unborn of the accusation of the murder of my child, both me and my husband. I wish I was closer to him when he was struck, and I would have been murdered before he was.*

The CORONER: *Have you been able to find out anything connected with your son's death?*
Answer: *No, but I hope before I die I may find who has murdered my boy.*

At the conclusion of the mother's evidence the Inquiry was again adjourned until 6 pm on Thursday, 12 May 1870.

Although a further eight witnesses were called to give evidence on the final day of the Inquiry, the evidence of three people in particular was of a nature that appeared to be extremely prejudicial to the cause of the boy's parents. The first of these witnesses, and one whose evidence was perhaps the most damning heard throughout the whole Inquiry, was that given by William Craig, a young lad who had been a friend of the murdered boy. After confirming that he knew the deceased and was aware that he had been missing from home for several days, the Coroner moved on to ask him what he knew about the stories that the deceased's younger brother Sammy had been telling people about the murder:

The CORONER: *Has Sammy ever told you how Johnny was killed?*
Answer: *I was up at the fair a day or two after the body was found, and Sammy told me that his father had killed Johnny, and his*

mother held him, and that they put him in a sack and brought him up to the pit and covered him with their fingers.

Question: *Did Sammy say he had seen this or had been told of it?*
Answer: *He did not say either.*

Question: *Do you know whether Johnny was afraid of going home at other times?*
Answer: *Yes. About a week before he was killed he told me he was afraid to go home for fear he should get a beating.*

Question: *Did he say who he was afraid of being beaten by?*
Answer: *Yes, by his mother.*

Question: *Did he ever tell you that he had been beaten?*
Answer: *Yes, about a month before his death – he showed me his back, and it was blue.*

Question: *Did he say who had beaten him?*
Answer: *Yes, his mother.*

Question: *You say that Sammy told you that his father had killed Johnny, what made him say it to you? Had you said anything to him about it?*
Answer: *No, he called me to him and said, 'Bill, do you know who killed my brother?' I said, 'Who?' and he said, 'My father and mother.'*

A JUROR: *How old is Sammy?*
The CORONER: *He is five years of age, and was not called this week.*

Another witness whose testimony was contradictory of that given by the dead boy's mother was William Calvesbert who swore on oath that he had seen Mrs Harding walking down Golden Noble Hill, from the direction of the sandpit, at a quarter to six on the morning of the day that her son's body was found. Previous to this she had maintained that she had not been out of her house before half past eight on that particular morning. But it was the evidence of one of her immediate neighbours, a single woman named Mary Ann Marriage, which suggested that the parents had indeed been in the habit of beating their children:

The house in which I live adjoins the Hardings' house. There is only a wooden partition between the two houses, and my bedroom is next to the bedroom of the Hardings. One Sunday morning about two months ago I heard one of the boys shrieking 'Murder!' and being beaten. I opened my cupboard door, rapped and said 'You had better leave off.' The mother then said, 'Harding, you had better leave off beating him.' I cannot say which of the children it was that was being beaten, but I have heard them being beaten on other occasions.

The final cause for excitement in the crowded courtroom was when George Harding, the boy's father, was finally called to the witness-box. Once again the Coroner told him that he was not obliged to answer any questions that may tend to incriminate him, or make any other statement. He then asked Mr Harding if he wished to make any statement:

I have no statement to make, only.... [interrupted by the Coroner]
The CORONER: *If you wish to make any statement it must be upon oath and I must take it down.*
The FATHER: *Then I have no statement to make.*
The FOREMAN: *Are we allowed to ask this man any questions?*
The CORONER: *I think not. If he says anything it must be upon oath, and he does not wish to make any statement.*

The Coroner then told Mr Harding that he could leave the box.

After the remaining witnesses had given their evidence, the Coroner began his summing up for the Jury. He restated the facts of the case, remarking that from Monday night till between two and three on Tuesday afternoon (a period of seventeen hours) there was an entire blank. There was clear evidence that the mother was looking for her son on Monday night, and that she determined, to the annoyance of her husband, not to go to bed until she found him. But there was no evidence, however, that she did go out, or that the father did so. The medical evidence pointed to the fact that the deceased was killed in the early hours of Tuesday morning. This was, therefore, a serious matter for their consideration – there being a blank – and they must consider whether there was any evidence to fill that void.

The Coroner also made note of the fact that the mother had stated that she had not left the house until half past eight in the morning, whereas this was contradicted by a witness who said that he met her coming from the direction of the sandpit at a quarter to six. He further reminded them of some of the more positive points of the case, including the fact that the body had indeed been found dead in the pit and that someone must have covered him with sand to conceal the body from public view. And here again there was another blank in that there was no evidence as to any person having been seen near the pit at the time in question.

And with those words fixed firmly in their minds the Jury retired to consider their verdict. In the meantime there was an excited buzz of conversation within the court as the outcome of the case was eagerly awaited. After just one hour of deliberation the Jury made their way back into court. A breathless silence now pervaded the courtroom as the Coroner addressed the Jury:

The CORONER: *Have you agreed gentlemen?*
The FOREMAN: *We have, Sir. We have given this case our most serious consideration, and we find that the deceased was Wilfully Murdered, but sufficient evidence has not been produced to show by whom.*
The CORONER: *In legal phraseology that is a verdict of Wilful Murder against some person, or persons unknown. And this inquiry is concluded.*

As soon as the verdict had been delivered the spectators hurried from the court and for some time afterwards an angry crowd prevailed in the street outside. When Mr and Mrs Harding left the building they were greeted with so much taunting and shouting from the crowd, that they had to seek protection from a number of police officers who then proceeded to escort them home. Even so, they were followed and hooted at by a large number of people, mainly women, who were only dispersed with some difficulty.

And this is where this intriguing saga comes to an end. It would seem that the Harding family may have eventually moved away from the area, perhaps even from the country itself, as no trace of them can be found in any of the later census records. Of course, they may simply have changed their name in an attempt to escape any bad feeling which may have been directed towards them. But whatever the truth of the matter, the question still remains as to who killed John Harding.

CHAPTER 7

A Curious Case of Stabbing at Brightlingsea
1871

... it would seem that William Davis went up behind where Everett was standing and... stabbed him in the groin with a small knife.

As far as the people of Brightlingsea were concerned, the twin brothers William and James Davis were a decidedly odd couple. They had been born in nearby Alresford in 1827 and had spent most of their lives in each other's company. They lived together, worked together and socialised together, shunning any other close form of human contact. In appearance, they were small slight men with thin wrinkled faces and piercing blue eyes. They dressed in identical clothing and with their shoulder length hair and thickly bearded faces, they looked like a strange kind of double act as they walked around the town, with one twin always remaining a few feet behind the other. As might be expected, they were viewed with some derision by some of the locals who thought that they were a 'little touched', and the pair would often find themselves on the receiving end of all manner of cruel jibes and taunts.

From their early days they had earned their living as fishermen, working mostly in the Brightlingsea estuary and surrounding creeks and marshes where they would no doubt have eked out a living from the rich supply of oysters and other shellfish. By the 1870s they had acquired a small fishing smack named *Odd Times* which also doubled as their home throughout most of the week while they were engaged with their fishing activities. At weekends they would return to Brightlingsea to sell their catch and then return to their Alresford home to spend a day or two with their sister, Mary, before returning to their boat the following week. They would usually also find time at this juncture to seek a little liquid refreshment in some of the bars and inns of Brightlingsea where they would often end up rather the worse for wear, inviting yet more abuse and ridicule. In fact, it was during one such visit to the *Ship Inn* in Brightlingsea on the evening of Friday, 3 March 1871 that was to result in one of the twins being charged with attempted murder.

They arrived at the inn some time around eleven o'clock having been drinking at a number of other venues in the town beforehand. Consequently, when they turned up at the *Ship* they were a little noisy and boisterous, much to the annoyance of some of the other customers. After ordering a couple of quarts of beer and handing it round to some of the company present, they got themselves into an argument with a man named William Everett who had been drinking in the inn sometime before the twins arrived. The result of this altercation was that William Davis and Everett agreed to toss a coin to see who would pay for the drinks. Everett lost the bet and was apparently a little reluctant to pay his dues. Meanwhile, Davis began to annoy him by asking if he was going to cry because he had lost a pot of beer, and saying that he had no money, or would not have any if he was to pay all his debts in Brightlingsea. The result was that Everett threw his glass of beer into Davis's face and offered to fight them both if they did not stop annoying him.

The building seen on the left is the Ship Inn *where the stabbing of William Everett took place. During the First World War the inn was used for billeting Australian engineers and was described by one of their number as 'A champion billet and a cure for all ills'.* Alf Wakeling

Things finally began to quieten down and some of those present, including Everett and the twins, retired into another room where there was some music and dancing and remained there for the next hour or so. In due course, Everett decided that he needed to go outside and was followed shortly afterwards by the twins. Exactly what happened next is not clear but it would seem that William Davis went up behind where Everett was standing and, just as the latter was in the process of turning round, stabbed him in the groin with a small knife. He then walked off into the darkness to catch up with his brother who had walked on ahead. For a moment Everett was not sure what had happened but after becoming aware that he was bleeding called out to the landlord saying that he had been stabbed. A doctor was sent for and his wound was dressed. Although his injuries were not life threatening they were bad enough to confine him to his bed for the best part of a month.

The following day William Davis was arrested by Police Constable Trubshoe of Brightlingsea and remanded in custody to appear before the Magistrates. When told of the reason for his arrest and with what he was being charged, he said 'I am very sorry; he should have let me alone; it was all his own fault.'

Petty Sessions,

COLCHESTER (DIVISION), MARCH 18.
(Before C. H. Hawkins, C. R. Bree, M.D., H. Bingley, J. W. Lay, W. Macandrew, and W. H. Penrose Esqrs.; Captain Disney, and Rev. W. Walsh.)

Dr. Bree proposed that Mr. Hawkins take the chair, which was agreed to.

Unlawful Wounding at Brightlingsea.

William Davis, mariner, of Brightlingsea, was charged upon remand, with having, on the night of the 3rd inst., at Brightlingsea, unlawfully and maliciously wounded one William Everett, mariner, of the same place, by stabbing him with a knife, with the intention of doing him grievous bodily harm.

A press cutting from 18 March 1871 showing William Davis's first appearance at the county magistrates' court. Author's collection

Davis appeared before the County Magistrates on Saturday, 18 March where he was charged with maliciously wounding William Everett, mariner, by stabbing him with a knife, with the intention of doing him grievous bodily harm. A number of witnesses were called to give evidence, although the victim himself was too ill to attend. Surprisingly, one of the witnesses for the prosecution was James Davis, the prisoner's brother, who after stating that he was a mariner living at Alresford, made the following statement:

> *About eleven o'clock on the night of Friday, 3 March, I and my brother went into the Ship public house at Brightlingsea, and I saw William Everett there. I went away from the house first, before my brother, and walked on ahead. I saw no more of Everett. Afterwards my brother overtook me in the lane and we walked to our boat, and went on board. The next morning, about nine o'clock, we went home. As we were going home he told me he expected that he had cut the man who threw the beer into his face last night, but he did not know. The knife produced is my brother's – the prisoner's.*

At the conclusion of the proceedings, and with the defence deciding to reserve their evidence, the prisoner was committed for trial at the next assizes, at Chelmsford. Mr A E Church, appearing for the defence, asked that the prisoner be granted bail as the assizes would not be held until July next, and stating that the prisoner greatly regretted the occurrence. However, the Chairman said that the Bench were of the unanimous opinion that bail could not be taken.

The case was finally heard at the Assize court at Chelmsford on Thursday, 13 July 1871, when William Davis was charged on two separate counts of stabbing William Everett. A third count of stabbing – with intent to murder – was rejected by the Grand Jury. The prisoner was led into the court and took his place in the dock. He was forty-five-years-old, although he had the bewildered look of a frightened child who had been in trouble without really knowing the reason why. And as the proceedings got under way, he was constantly glancing around the court with an increasing look of terror in his eyes. His main focus in the crowd of faces, however, was that belonging to his twin brother James, who appeared to be just as terrified as his brother in the dock.

The first witness called was the victim of the crime, William Everett, who confirmed that he was a mariner living at Brightlingsea. He was then directed by his counsel to relate to the court his version of events on the evening in question:

> On the 3 March I was at the Ship Inn at Brightlingsea, and went there about half-past ten. I saw the prisoner and his brother there and we tossed for a pot of beer, which I lost. The beer was put on the table and I told Mr Cooper, the landlord, that I would pay for it. The prisoner then began to annoy me and asked me if I was going to cry because I had lost a pot of beer. He also said that the clothes which I had on were not paid for, and he kept jeering at me. I then took up a small glass of beer that was standing on the table and part of it went on to the prisoner's face. I said, 'Now be quiet and don't interfere with me anymore.' I did not open my mouth to abuse him, nor did I offer to fight him and his brother. I afterwards went into another room where there was a concertina and dancing going on. After we had been dancing for about an hour I went out for a necessary purpose. The prisoner and his brother, who had also been in the room where there was dancing, followed me out. During the time that I was out I saw the prisoner's brother passing me. Afterwards as I was in the act of turning round I saw the prisoner standing beside me and he immediately stabbed me in my private parts. He then made off and I could feel the blood running down my legs. I went back to the pub and said, 'Cooper, I am stabbed.' He then helped me into the house and afterwards put me to bed. A doctor was sent for and came soon afterwards. I was confined to bed at the Ship for about a fortnight and was then removed to my own house, where I remained in bed for about a month.

The next witness called was Thomas Cooper, landlord of the *Ship Inn*, whose evidence mirrored that given by the prosecutor, William Everett. He did, however, add that the prisoner and his brother had both been the worse for drink when they had arrived at his house, whilst Everett had been perfectly sober. Other witnesses called to give evidence included the arresting constable, PC Trubshoe, who told the court that he had known the prisoner for about twenty years and had never known him to be in trouble before, and the surgeon, Mr William Squire Ling, who attended the victim shortly after the stabbing. He described in great detail the nature of the wound inflicted upon the victim, but concluded that his injuries no longer presented any danger.

Mr Croome, counsel for the prisoner, then addressed the Jury for the defence and contended that at the time of the stabbing the prisoner was too intoxicated to have had any intention of disabling or wounding the prosecutor. In further mitigation, he stated that his client's actions were the result of extreme provocation which he had received whilst in the house, and also that he feared that the prosecutor (William Everett) had been about to attack him.

His Lordship then summarised the case for the benefit of the Jury and stated that there should be no doubt as to whether or not the prisoner had actually stabbed the prosecutor, but rather whether or not the prisoner should be convicted of stabbing with intent to do grievous bodily harm, or simply that of unlawful wounding. After retiring to ponder these points, the Jury returned a verdict of guilty with intent to do grievous bodily harm. His Lordship, in passing sentence, said that it was a most savage, cruel, unprovoked and deliberate crime that the prisoner had been found guilty of, and he did not think – indeed he knew - he should not be performing his duty if he did not pass a very severe sentence. He accordingly sentenced the prisoner to five years penal servitude.

Both the prisoner in the dock and his brother sitting in the court appeared dumbstruck at the severity of the sentence. They seemed dazed and when the prisoner was led away from the court his brother's eyes followed him with an even deeper look of despair and helplessness. According to the order of things, the prisoner would then have been returned to the convict gaol at Springfield where he would have served out his sentence before being reunited with his brother some five years later. Certainly, at the time of the 1881 census the brothers were back living on their fishing smack doing what they knew best. They are still there in 1891, but by 1901 they seem to have vanished. And this is where the story might have ended had it not been for the presence of another person who was present in court on the day that William was convicted. This person had no connection with the case in question, but was part of a legal team which had assembled to work on another case due to be heard later in the day. The individual concerned was Mr F Curruthers Gould, a young barrister, who was about to embark upon his first legal case. Having arrived at court in plenty of time he had decided to sit through the preceding case in the hope of learning a trick or two from some of his more experienced peers. However, he was soon to become transfixed in the events which were unravelling before him, so much so that he ended up feeling quite sympathetic to the poor defendant's plight. After the prisoner was taken down, however, his memory of the occasion began to fade and may have disappeared from his memory altogether had it not been for a chance encounter some twenty-five years later.

This event took place whilst Mr Gould, by now an attorney of some standing, was engaged in the shooting of wildfowl on the River Blackwater during the winter of 1896. It was a foggy morning, he recalled, as he sailed his small punt along the estuary close to the village of Bradwell when all of a sudden he noticed a battered looking old fishing smack lying in the mud and decided to investigate:

'There was no one on deck, but a thin wisp of blue smoke was curling up from somewhere on board', he said. The craft looked so old and weather-worn that my curiosity was aroused, and I went alongside and hailed, 'Anybody aboard here?' Presently, a queer strange little old withered face, framed with tangled wisps of yellowish-white hair, peered at me from the fore-hatch.

'Are you living on board this craft?' I asked. But there was no reply, a pair of bleared and watery light blue eyes stared at me with a puzzled, hunted expression which seemed to awaken some chord of memory in my mind. 'Do you want any baccy?' I asked, for I noticed that although there was a little black clay

pipe between the old man's lips, it was not alight. There was a sudden hungry gleam in the pale eyes which answered my question without the need of words. The mention of tobacco had a still more singular effect, for presently another and a duplicate face peered up alongside the first. They were so much alike that it quite startled me as some thing uncanny.

I had a spare tobacco pouch in my pocket and I tossed it up on board, telling the men they might take it all. Two thin claw-like hands shot out and clutched the treasure. I asked some questions and the two poor old fellows, thawing under the anticipation of the coming smoke, answered me timidly in squeaky little voices. They lived on board by themselves, they told me, and they rarely went ashore anywhere. They didn't care to, they said, and as they spoke there was a frightened look in the two pairs of eyes which glanced hurriedly and nervously towards the land, as if they dreaded something there.

There was still that haunting chord of memory ringing in my brain. Surely, I fancied, I must have seen these two men before, but I could not call to mind how, and when, and where. However, I had to get back to my punt before the tide turned, so I bade the crew of the solitary boat goodbye, but not until I had thrown them one of the geese which I had shot, adding that, 'The butcher doesn't call here often, I expect?'

As I turned round once to look back, those two queer little faces were still above the fore-hatch watching me. A day or two afterwards I was sailing through the Main on a high tide, and seeing the old smack I steered in close. Just as I was passing her, I was hailed by two shrill little voices, and there were the two old men holding out something in their hands and beckoning to me.

I brought up alongside, and found that they had got half a dozen fine oysters, which they told me they had dredged up and had kept for me fresh in water on the chance of seeing me again. Poor old fellows; it was all they could give me, and I need hardly say that I was more proud of those half dozen natives than if I had been a fellow guest at a Colchester Oyster Feast with the Lord Mayor and Sheriffs of London.

William and James Davis aboard their fishing smack Odd Times.
Anonymous - Essex Review, vol 8, 1899

Later in the day when Mr Gould had returned to his Brightlingsea hotel he was told something of the story of the old men whom he had seen on the lonely mudflats. As the story began to unfold, that scene in the courtroom at Chelmsford all those years ago came flashing back to his mind.   He listened intently and was particularly interested in finding out how it was that they came to be living all alone in their old boat out on that desolate spot. He was told that when one of the brothers was sent to prison his twin brother had set to work in a desperate attempt to get his sentence shortened. He had spent what little store of money he had going to and fro begging and imploring magistrates, clergymen – even the Home Secretary himself, to let his brother out. And at last some kindly people, who had found out the truth of the case, decided to intervene on his behalf with the result that his brother was released. From this time on the brothers seem to have disappeared almost entirely, preferring the desolate existence out on the flats far away from all traces of human society which they had good cause to dread.

CHAPTER 8

The Fordham Double Murder
1875

...Thomas had temporarily taken leave of his senses ...

All crimes involving the deliberate taking of another person's life may be regarded as equally abhorrent, regardless of the type of crime committed, or indeed, the motive. But even within the broad framework of murder types, some crimes are regarded as being even more abhorrent than others - and these include the killing of one's own children or indeed one's parents. The case which we are now going to examine fits firmly into this category and resulted in what has become known as 'The Fordham Double Murder.'

The village of Fordham lies about six miles north west of Colchester, just off the main road to Halstead, and is named after the crossing of the River Colne in what is today known as Ford Street. The present community numbers about 800 and despite having a strong agricultural feel about the place, very few of its inhabitants are employed on the land, or indeed work in the village itself. But back in 1875, when the particular crime in question was committed, almost every other adult male was employed in farm work, mostly as agricultural labourers. One of these individuals was Thomas Johnson, a thirty-eight-year-old agricultural labourer who lived with his elderly parents, Solomon and Susannah, in a small treble-tenanted cottage at the edge of the village. Thomas was the youngest of three children born to Solomon and Susannah – the elder two, Mary (b.1819) and Henry (b.1821) were some years older than Thomas who was born in 1836. The younger son had never married and was apparently devoted to looking after his elderly parents – that is until the morning of Saturday, 20 March 1875.

The family had apparently woken early on that particular weekend morning – they were certainly up and about before seven o'clock – but within minutes of that hour passing a crime of horrifying magnitude had taken place which was to shake the very heart of the community and provide a topic for local gossip for decades to come. For while most of the village of Fordham was still slumbering an intense argument had broken out within the Johnson household which was to result in the brutal slaying of the elderly couple. For reasons that may never be fully realised, Thomas had temporarily taken leave of his senses and battered his terrified mother and father to death with a poker and shovel. Neighbours who lived in the adjoining cottages managed to raise the alarm and Thomas was eventually apprehended and taken into custody. By twelve o'clock that same morning the assailant was standing before the County Magistrates sitting in Petty Session at Colchester Town Hall.

After having committed the terrible crime Johnson had taken off towards the centre of the village after having threatened one of his neighbours, a Mrs Eliza Mills, who had witnessed the entire event. In fact, at the height of the assault Mrs Mills had sent her young son about a mile up the road to

The Three Horse Shoes *public house at Fordham as seen in about 1910.   This was where the inquest was held into the cause of Solomon and Susannah Johnson's tragic death at the hands of their deranged son, Thomas.* Fordham Local History Society

the public house for assistance, but by the time help was on its way, in the form of local blacksmith, Jubal Partridge, and Jonathan Sparkes, it was too late to save them. As the pair made their way down the road they came face to face with Johnson as he walked from the scene of the crime. After a few words had passed between the three of them a brief scuffle ensued during which time Johnson, who was still armed with the poker with which he had bludgeoned his parents, struck out at Partridge several times hitting him twice on the arm. As the struggle continued Johnson said to them that he had the power of God Almighty and that he was to kill all whom he met. However, Partridge and Sparkes finally got the better of him and after strapping him up took him to the *Three Horse Shoes* public house. He was later conveyed to the Union Workhouse at Stanway from where he was taken into custody by Police Constable Charles Richardson from Stanway.

But now standing in front of the magistrates at the Town Hall Johnson had quietened down and had a subdued manner

Part of the former Lexden and Winstree Union Workhouse where Thomas Johnson was taken after being apprehended. The workhouse later became St Albright's hospital but is now used for office accommodation. The Author

about him. He was thirty-eight years old and described as having a dark complexion with a bushy black beard and whiskers. His hands and face (which were still smeared with blood) still bore traces of the dreadful act which he had just committed, and of his struggle with the men who had apprehended him. However, despite his rather wild appearance, he managed to maintain his composure during this brief examination and answered all the questions put to him. When asked by the Clerk of the Court (Mr Jones) what particular business he followed, he replied: 'I am in no business at all – I am a horseman, that is my occupation when I am at work.' He also confirmed that his father's name was Solomon and his mother's Susannah. He was then charged with the wilful killing of them both at Fordham and remanded in custody until the following Wednesday. He was then removed from the court and conveyed by cab to the County Police Station on Ipswich Road.

On the following Monday, Mr William Good, Coroner for North Essex, held an inquest at the *Three Horseshoes Inn* at Fordham. After the usual formalities had been gone through, Mr Good read a letter received from Superintendent Daunt under whose authority the prisoner had been remanded since the earlier hearing. It stated that since the prisoner had been held in confinement at the County Gaol, he had become very violent and outrageously mad and that in his opinion it would be unwise and dangerous to allow him to attend the inquest. The Coroner agreed that no benefit would be gained from having the prisoner present, particularly as there was direct evidence of his having committed the crime, and he was well-known to the witnesses. The Jury then proceeded to view the bodies of the deceased couple and the scene where they met their deaths.

The case was well reported in the local press and the following selected extracts, taken from a series of reports published in the *Essex Standard* newspaper, will allow the reader to gain a much better idea of the atmosphere of the occasion:

Mrs. Eliza Mills, wife of a labourer, was the first witness called – I lived next door to the deceased Solomon and Susannah Johnson. The former was 80 years of age - 81 next April, and the latter was about 79 years, according to what she has told me.

The CORONER: *Did they live alone?*
Answer: *Yes, with the exception of the son who did this deed.*
Question: *And you live under the same roof?*
Answer: *Yes.*
Question: *Now we come to the facts. Did you see the son on Friday night?*
Answer: *Yes, between seven and eight o'clock on Friday night, he came to his father's house; I saw him in the garden, and he said 'Good night' to me; I only caught a glimpse of him.*
Question: *Now as to next morning?*
Answer: *Well, I went to bed at night and never heard anything until seven o'clock in the morning.*
Question: *Well what happened then?*
Answer: *I was standing in my room with my little boy, when we heard Thomas Johnson call out to his mother, 'Go down you wi----, what are you looking at me for, I'll kill you.' Almost immediately after, Mrs. Johnson came into my house and said to me, 'Oh I say dear neighbour what shall I do; he,* [meaning her son] *says he'll kill me.' I told her to 'Give him into charge.'*
Question: *She said; 'Who can I send?'*
Answer: *I said, 'My little boy is here, and I will send him for assistance,' I did not know where to send, but I sent him up to the public house. She went back into her house and finished dressing; but before my child could get far up the road, Thomas Johnson drove the two deceased out of the house into the garden. He followed them out into the garden.*
Question: *Had he anything in his hand then?*
Answer: *No, not then but he returned immediately, and came out again with the poker. Then he struck the poor old man several times.*
Question: *Were they running away in the garden?*
Answer: *No; the poor old man followed him, and his son then struck him several times across his shoulder, until he fell into an ashpit in the garden.*
Mr. JONES: *Did you hear anything?*
Answer: *Yes; the poor old gentleman called to me.*
The CORONER: *Well, what next?*

Answer: *After the poor old gentleman fell into the ash-pit, he struck him on the head with the poker.*

Question: *Where were you at this time?*

Answer: *At my door, where I could see all that was going on. I said to him, 'Tommy you will kill your father and mother' and he said, 'Yes, I will kill them, the old ------.' He then ran to his mother.*

Question: *Did he not strike his father more than once in the ashpit?*

Answer: *Not then. I will tell you presently. He then ran to his mother and struck her with the poker across the shoulder several times.*

Question: *Did it knock her down?*

Answer: *Yes, she was down when I saw her.*

Question: *Did he strike her again afterwards?*

Answer: *Yes, several times. She was sitting down, and put her hands up and said, 'Oh Tommy, you'll kill me.'*

Question: *Where did he strike her?*

Answer: *On the arms and head. I then ran for assistance to the nearest cottage that I could come to. I felt as if I could not run any further, and the woman came out for assistance.*

Mr. JONES: *And then you went back?*

Answer: *Yes, and I went back across Mr. Green's field to my cottage - It was out of my path, but I knew Mr. Green would not mind that, when I heard Thomas Johnson say 'You may run; I'll kill you you old ------. You may run; I'll kill you.' I did not see him for I was so frightened that I could not look at him, but I heard him.*

Question: *Did he follow you?*

Answer: *No, for I suppose the men happened on him directly. I then returned home and found my poor neighbour [Mrs Johnson] sitting near the well in the garden, smothered in blood.*

Question: *Was she sensible?*

Answer: *Yes, very.*

Question: *What did she say?*

Answer: *She said to me, 'My dear neighbour, come to me.'*

Question: *What did you say?*

Answer: *I said. 'I will in a minute, dear, but I am afraid he is after me.' I then went in and locked my door for a few minutes, for I was afraid he was after me. Finding he did not come, I went and led her into my house. She sat a few minutes and then said 'Lead me into* *my house, dear, for I shall die.' She also said, 'Oh my poor back and head, what shall I do, dear?' I then led her into her house, and sat her in the chair, after which she walked across the other side of the room. Shortly afterwards I was taking her husband's cushion away, and she said, 'Don't, perhaps he'll come in in a minute;' She also said, 'Where's my dear old man?' I did not like to tell her he was dead, although I knew he was, for I had been and looked.*

Question: *When did you go and look at him?*

Answer: *Directly I had led his wife into her house. She asked me several times where he was and asked me if he was dead. I did not like to tell her and merely said, 'He is outside.'*

Question: *When did she die?*

Answer: *In about two hours - at about nine by their clock, but that might have been a little too fast.*

Question: *Did she say anything about Tommy?*

Answer: *No, she asked me 'Who has done this to me?' and I said, 'Tommy;' upon which she said, 'Well, I don't think he knew it, then.'*

The CORONER: *I don't suppose the woman knew what she was saying, for she had previously said, 'You'll kill me Tommy.'*

Having completed her evidence Mrs Mills was asked to stand down. The next witness called was her granddaughter, Emma Campin, aged eleven years, who lived in the house with her:

I was in my grandmother's house on Saturday morning about seven o'clock and was looking out of the window while my grandmother was away. I saw Thomas Johnson knock his father and mother about with a shovel on the head and shoulders, he kept going backwards and forwards to them. I saw him go from one to the other about six times. The old gentleman was in the ashpit at that time. He kept going backwards and forwards, striking them each time with the shovel.

The CORONER: *A wonderful thing that after this, the woman should have lived so long.*

Mr. JONES: *Yes, it is most astonishing.*

Witness (continuing): *'He then went and got the poker, and came and broke my grandmother's windows, and said he would kill us. We*

all ran upstairs.'
Question: *What did he say?*
Answer: *He said he would kill all of us in the house.* [There were two other children in the house].
Question: *Did you see what became of him at last?*
Answer: *He then left the premises with the poker on his shoulders and walked up the road. I saw no more of him.*
[Witness identified the shovel, which was produced. There were some blood stains on it, and a hair, which Sergt. Raven said was from the female deceased's head].

Mr Charles Jack Worts, surgeon, from Fordham, was then called to give evidence:

> *I was called to see the deceased on Saturday morning about eight o'clock. I arrived there about half-past eight. I first saw the man, who was lying in the dust bin on his right side with his head bent forward. I examined the wounds and found the occipital and parietal bones were both smashed. It appeared to have been done with the edge of a shovel. There was also a gash on the forehead. The brain was protruding from the wound. There were other wounds, but they were matted with blood and hair and I did not examine for fractures, as it would have been impossible to tell the extent of the fractures without a post-mortem examination. The injuries to the occipital and parietal bones were sufficient to account for death. On examining the body of the woman, who, I was told, had only died a very few minutes earlier, I found a large gash across the top part of the head, and the posterior part was battered in. There were other severe wounds about the head, but I did not examine for fractures. The wounds were covered with blood.*

The Coroner remarked that they might have been washed. Mr Worts said that he knew the woman was dead and supposed the murderer to be still at large, and, fearing that he might do further mischief, went in search of him and found that he had been captured. In reply to further questions, the witness said there were other wounds on the head of a severe character and he attributed death to compression of the brain, the result of the fracture.

The CORONER: *Don't you think it marvellous the poor woman lived so long?*

Mr Worts said that it was marvellous, but then went on to explain how she could have lived so long.

After deciding that it was not necessary to call any further witnesses the Coroner summarised the proceedings. He said that he thought there could be little or no doubt that the unfortunate victims died from injuries inflicted by their son, the prisoner Thomas Johnson, and not only was there direct and positive evidence to point to that conclusion, but there was the man's own confession, and under those circumstances he concluded they could only come to one conclusion - that the man was guilty of wilful murder. There was every reason to believe that the murderer was in a state of mental aberration, but the state of his mind was not for them to inquire into, that being a matter which would be sifted and decided upon at another place. He thought no further observations were required from him and that if the Jury were satisfied with the evidence, it would be their duty to return a verdict of wilful murder against Thomas Johnson. After a very brief consultation, the Foreman said the Jury had not the slightest hesitation in bringing in that verdict. The prisoner was then bound over to appear at the forthcoming Assize Court at Chelmsford.

On the following Wednesday, 31 March 1875, the prisoner Thomas Johnson was again brought before the County Magistrates at the Town Hall for further examination. He arrived at the court in a cab shortly after half-past eleven and a large crowd had congregated outside to witness his arrival. The prisoner, who was seated during the examination, presented an even more wild appearance than when brought before the Magistrates on Saturday, shortly after committing the murder, and he was carefully guarded by two constables. The main witnesses repeated their evidence as given to the Coroner earlier, although on this occasion Johnson was present in the courtroom and was allowed to ask questions. As Mrs Mills was being examined by the magistrates, Johnson was becoming more and more agitated and was displaying signs of religious mania and madness. After hearing Mrs Mills say that the last time she had seen the prisoner before the tragic occurrence was on Friday evening, he remarked, 'That was when God first called me by His grace, manifestly.' He also pointed to the little girl Campin and said, 'That is the little damsel that has been playing the harp; her mother is risen from the dead.' He also stated that he had told his parents years ago that he would kill them, and accused Mrs Mills of having taken his inside out, as well as several other wild statements.

At length the Chairman of the magistrates told the prisoner that he could now ask Mrs Mills any questions concerning her evidence:

Prisoner: *Have you anything to say about me, Mrs. Mills.*
Witness: *No, Tommy, nothing more than I have already said; you have always been a good child to your poor old people, and they have been good parents to you.*
Prisoner: *Not so very kind the latter part of the time. What did they bewitch me for?*
Witness: *I don't know about that.*
Prisoner: *I have not much to say. I believe what she says is very right and very true.*

Emma Campin, granddaughter of the last witness, also repeated her previous evidence before Johnson was again asked if he would like to ask the witness any questions. After saying that he had no mind to ask this witness any questions, he looked up to the gallery above him and shouted out several times 'Praise Him ye noble army of martyrs; praise Him; praise Him.'

When Mr Worts, the surgeon, was giving his evidence to the magistrates and stating that he had arrived at the scene of the crime at about nine o'clock, Johnson interrupted him and said that it was seven o'clock...

The Chairman interrupted and explained that the witness was not speaking of the time when, as he (the prisoner) said, he did the deed.

Prisoner: *Yes, he is. Don't tell a lie; hold your tongue; I am not* *going to have my father's name blasphemed, but will fight up to my knees in blood for him; I will slay them one at a time, and spear them; I'll put a ring through your nose, and you shall have a six and fifty on you; I'll bore it myself.*

The CHAIRMAN: *Do you wish to ask Mr Worts any questions?*
Prisoner: *No, I have no mind to ask him anything.* [To Mr. Worts]. *You old scamp; get down; what did you do to my head? You withered it didn't you; get down.*

The chairman asked the prisoner to keep himself quiet for a few minutes.

Prisoner: *Who are you? It's old Papillon from Lexden; I don't fear you; I shall do God's justice.*
The CHAIRMAN: *That is quite right; then you will keep quiet; that will be one way of doing justice.*
Prisoner: *I shall when I like; I shall not be ruled by you; I shall talk as long as I like, and you can help yourself. We'll see if my power is not the strongest.*

After all the evidence had been presented the prisoner was formerly charged with the murders and was asked if he would like to make a formal statement. He said that he did and went on to say that he wanted to destroy the Devil's kingdom and to build up God Almighty's. While the Clerk was taking down the statement Johnson continued to make a series of strange and incoherent remarks. Having signed the statement the Chairman informed him that he would be sent to Springfield gaol at Chelmsford to await his trial at the next Assize:

Prisoner: *Oh, the Assizes. When do they commence? In March, I think.*
The CHAIRMAN: *No, in July.*
Prisoner: *Oh, I thought it was in March. Don't tell me any lies. You are a liar.*

He was continuing in this manner when the Constables spoke to him and quietened him down. He was then removed from the courtroom to a waiting cab and taken to the railway station, and then on to Chelmsford by the 2.14 pm train.

By the time that the case was due to be heard at the Essex Summer Assize at Chelmsford on 16 July 1875, Johnson had already been committed to Broadmoor Criminal Lunatic Asylum. No doubt his mental condition had deteriorated whilst in custody and the record shows that a warrant for his committal was authorised by The Right Honorable Richard Ashton Goss (Principal Secretary of State) on 8 April 1875. The case was accordingly postponed *Sine Die* (indefinitely). The nature of his mental disorder, from which he failed to recover, was noted as chronic delusional insanity, and he died in Broadmoor on 29 October 1911.

At the inquest held on 31 October 1911, the cause of death was recorded as 'inflammation of the brain.' The bodies of his mother and father were laid to rest in Colchester Cemetery on 26 March 1875, with the following notation made at the foot of the burial register by the presiding clergyman: 'A husband and wife buried in the same grave. They were both killed at the same time (March 20th) by their son Thomas Johnson; a maniac with a poker and spade.'

In conclusion, it can be said that Thomas was in 'good company' during his confinement in Broadmoor – which, incidentally, was the first custom-built criminal lunatic asylum in the world. According to the 1881 census he shared his accommodation with 299 other men and 95 women, and as might be expected the inmates came from all manner of social backgrounds. They included a number of people who were described as gentlemen, artists, surgeons and even one or two clergymen! Indeed, one of the artists listed was the famous Victorian painter Richard Dadd who specialised in painting scenes of fairies. Also listed is Dr William Chester Minor who was one of the leading contributors of quotations for the first *Oxford English Dictionary* – all researched during his period of incarceration.

Table 1: Some inmates at Broadmoor Criminal Lunatic Asylum in 1881

William GREENAWAY	W	Male	62	Petworth, Sussex	Castrator
William TUCHET	U	Male	59		Gentleman
John GOODE	U	Male	84		Chelsea Pensioner
Richard DADD	U	Male	63	Chatham, Kent	Artist
William CHESTER	U	Male	47	Ceylon	Surgeon
William JENKINS	W	Male	45	Newport, Monmouth	Baptist Minister
Thomas JOHNSON	**U**	**Male**	**34**	**Fordham, Essex**	**Agricultural Lab.**
Henry SMITH	U	Male	30	Shrewsbury, Shrop.	Tramp
Thomas NOYES	U	Male	53	Gorsdon, Hertford	Home Office Clerk
William BULL	M	Male	59		Sweep
Hannah FISK	M	Female	31	Colchester, Essex	Wife of a Seaman
Charlotte KING	M	Female	46	Liss, Hampshire	Wife of a Policeman

(Notice that Thomas Johnson's age has been incorrectly recorded – it should be 44.)

The Three Horse Shoes *public house as it appears today.* The Author

CHAPTER 9

Killed by a Raging Bull
1875

*... several large crashing noises were heard to
come from within the van...*

It is probably fair to say that most people are aware of the inherent dangers associated with bulls - certainly few people would be silly enough to enter a field containing one, let alone climb into a confined space with one knowing that it was likely to be highly stressed and agitated. But this is exactly what farm labourer, James King, did back in July 1875, with devastating consequences. The bull immediately charged at him breaking several of his ribs and crushing his liver, and although he was taken to the local hospital where everything possible was done for him, he died an agonising death some twenty hours later. But what were the events which led up to this tragic episode and, more importantly, why did James King put himself at such peril?

The beast which carried out the deadly attack was, in fact, a prize bull named 'Heydon Duke II' and was owned by Mr Daniel Green of Donyland Place, on the outskirts of Colchester. The bull had been purchased at the Royal Show in Hull some two years previously and was now, on the morning of Monday, 5 July 1875, about to be conveyed to the Essex Agricultural Show at Brentwood. The person in charge of taking the bull to the railway station at Colchester, and accompanying him to Brentwood, was forty-nine-year-old James King, who had been in Mr Green's employ as a stockman for about two years. For most of that time he had been in sole charge of the bull and entirely responsible for its management – and therefore well acquainted with the animal and used to handling him. After the bull had been loaded onto the van and secured to a bar by means of a halter round its head and by a line leading to a ring through its nose, they set off for the station sometime around a quarter past six.

At some stage during the early part of the journey the animal apparently became a little restive and when they arrived at Old Heath, close to the site of the *Health and Happiness* beer house, King decided to stop the van and investigate what the problem was. After climbing down from his seat he opened a small door at the side of the van to investigate and could immediately see what was wrong. The bull had apparently shifted a rail and he decided to climb in to put it right. From what witnesses later related at the Coroner's inquest, he never hesitated before climbing in, obviously confident that his charge was tame enough and presented no danger. This may, of course, have been the case in most other situations, but it would seem that he must have surprised the bull by unexpectedly entering the van at this point, and being unable to retreat from the perceived danger because of his restraint, the bull went for the only other option open to it and attacked him. Seconds after climbing in with the bull several loud crashing noises were heard to come from within the van, together with the terrified cries of James King as he was being crushed and knocked about by the bull. He had obviously made a serious error of judgement and was now to suffer the gravest of consequences.

A typical short-horn bull from around 1900. Author's collection

An official inquest into the cause of his death was held on Wednesday, 7 July in the Boardroom at the Essex and Colchester Hospital in Lexden Road before Mr Adolphus Church, the Coroner. In opening the proceedings, the Coroner spoke of the events which had led up to the tragedy and then called his first witness, Henry Tosbell, a shepherd who was also in the employ of Mr Green. Mr Tosbell confirmed that the deceased had been looking after the bull for about two years and had always accompanied it when it was sent to agricultural shows. He said that on Monday morning he had been present when the bull was being got ready for the journey and had even helped to lead the animal into the truck. He said that the bull went in very quietly and was tied to the rail by the deceased. The following series of questions were then put to the witness by the Coroner and members of the Jury:

The CORONER: *What kind of tempered animal was this bull?*
Answer: *It always appeared to be a very quiet animal.*
A JUROR: *What was its age?*
Answer: *About four years.*
The CORONER: *Had you ever seen it display any viciousness?*
Answer: *Never; I saw it every day, and I never saw it otherwise than quiet. I think the deceased tied the animal a little too low – he allowed it a little too much rope, so that it could lie down, which he encouraged it to do. I noticed this in the morning, but I did not say anything to him as I thought he knew better than I did, and he was going with it. If he had not allowed it so much rope it could not have thrown its head about. The truck in which the bull was being conveyed was a covered one, and both ends will let down for the purpose of allowing the animals to walk in and out. There is also a small trapdoor at one side just big enough to allow a man to get through.*

In reply to a remark by the Foreman of the Jury, the witness stated that he had frequently seen the bull take food from out of the deceased's hand, and that it appeared to be very fond of him.

The CORONER: *Was the place where the deceased entered the*

van the usual place to get in?
Answer: *No.*
Question: *How large was the aperture?*
Answer: *About a yard long and two feet wide.*
Question: *You would have trouble to get in?*
Answer: *I could get in very well.*
Question: *That is how you imagined the deceased got in?*
Answer: *Yes, and just where he got in was where the bull's head was. I would not have got in there for any money.*

The next witness called was Mrs Ann Humm, wife of a gardener, of Old Heath, who said that at about a quarter to seven on the morning in question she saw the deceased drive past and stop opposite the *Health and Happiness* beer house:

I was standing on my steps and I saw him get down from his seat and open the little door', she said. 'I thought that he was going to show the bull to Mr Brown, the landlord of the Health and Happiness. The deceased said that the animal had shifted a rail and that he must go in and put it right. I saw him get through the little door into the truck and then immediately heard him call out to the bull 'Go back.' I could see the bull from where I stood, and noticed that as soon as he had spoke, the bull moved as if striking at him, and then I heard a crash.

The CORONER: *Did he call out?*
Answer: *Not then.*
Question: *Did the bull do this more than once?*
Answer: *Oh yes, the first time the deceased did not call out, but the animal struck him a second time, and I called out to Mr Brown that the man would be killed. I also heard the deceased cry at the same time, 'I shall be killed.'*
Question: *How many times did the bull strike him?*
Answer: *Three or four times I should say. Mr Brown was standing against the little door, but he could not see so well as I could, as I was standing on higher ground. As soon as the deceased called out that he should be killed, Mr Brown said, 'Come out Jim, come out' but the animal struck him again, and Mr Brown, seeing that he could not get out by himself, pulled him out, tearing his slop [A type of*

loose outer garment] *in two as he did so. The deceased fell onto the grass when pulled out and I ran over to him and said, 'You are hurt Mr King', to which he replied, 'Take me to hospital.'*

The CORONER: *It was the deceased's own act in getting into the van?*

Answer: *Well, we may think him to blame.*

Question: *But it was his own act?*

Answer: *Yes.*

In reply to a question from a juror, the witness stated that she did not think that the horns of the bull had entered any part of the deceased's body, as she saw no sign of blood. She said that they immediately sent for Mr Green (the owner of the bull) who came at once and arranged for a cart to take him to the hospital. He also sent for his own medical man, Mr Partridge, who soon arrived and assisted in getting the poor man into the cart and off to the hospital.

John Brown, landlord of the *Health and Happiness* was then called to give his account of what happened. He began by stating that he was crossing the road near to his house at about

Fingringhoe Road looking north towards Old Heath Road, 2005. The Health and Happiness *beer house used to stand on the left side of the road near the line of parked cars.* The Author

a quarter to seven on Monday morning when the deceased drove up with the van and said, 'I think something is wrong, John – there is something amiss in the van – and I shall take a look.' He then saw the deceased open the little door at the side of the van and say, 'You old rascal (meaning the bull), you have pulled your rail down.' Mr Brown then saw the deceased climb into the van:

> *The deceased then took a short whip and jumped in saying, 'I don't like the look of him.' He held up his whip and said to the bull, 'Stand back' and he was instantly knocked down, although I didn't actually see the animal strike him. He then called out, 'I shall be killed', and I said 'Good God, come out James' and seeing that he could not get out, I caught hold of him and pulled him out by force. He said that he was dying and asked to be carried to the hospital.*

The owner of the bull, Mr Daniel Green, was then questioned about the bull's temperament and character:

> *I have had this bull for about two years, having purchased him from Lord Braybrooke's agent at the Royal Agricultural Show at Hull. I received a very good character with him and understood that he was quiet. I had seen him at several shows prior to buying him.*

The CORONER: *During the time the bull has been in your possession, has it been quiet?*
Answer: *Yes, and no more trouble than animals of that character generally are. Bulls always want great care. The deceased had been in the habit of attending to it regularly, and he has exercised it on Donyland Heath four or five days a week at least, and he has taken it to several agricultural shows. I was present when the animal was put into the truck on Monday morning. It was very quiet and walked into the van without any trouble.*
Question: *Did you notice the way in which it was tied up?*
Answer: *No. I wish I had looked how he had tied him but I did not.*
Question: *Was it not an injudicious thing for him to do – to get in as he did?*
Answer: *Most injudicious. He could not have done a more*

injudicious thing than to have got in suddenly by that door.
Question: *What effect would it probably have?*
Answer: *I should think that it would have upset the bull at once. I should have considered it was certain death to any man.*

A juror then once again asked the witness how he thought the animal had been tied:

'It had probably been tied to a single rail,' he said. 'And although that would have been contrary to the instructions which I had originally given to him, because he was so used to the bull, I would have allowed him to do what he thought best. I had originally told him that the bull should always be tied to the two sides of the van, so that his head would be kept as near as possible to the centre.'

The CORONER: *Although the rail may have been disturbed as stated, was there any necessity for the deceased to go into the van to put it right?*
Answer: *Not in the least. When I arrived, a man by my directions lifted the halter with a stick and put it right in as little time as it has taken me to tell it to you.*

The front view and main entrance to the Essex County Hospital in the early 1900s. The hospital was opened in 1820 and is still serving the needs of the community.
Jess Jephcott

Mr R M Boodle, House Surgeon at the Hospital, reported that the deceased was brought to that institution about nine o'clock on Monday morning and was at once removed to a ward and put to bed. Upon examination, he was found to be very faint from loss of blood, three or four of his ribs were broken, and there was air under the skin showing that the lung had been injured. The right wrist was also broken, the abdomen very much distended, and he complained of great pain. There were no puncture wounds and the loss of blood was internal. He received every attention at the hospital and Mr Symmons, the surgeon for the week, saw him at twelve o'clock. However, he got fainter, continued to vomit, and he died at three o'clock on Tuesday morning.

The Coroner explained that although he had not personally considered it necessary to order a post-mortem examination, he had asked the House Surgeon to perform one as the deceased's wife was anxious to know the extent of her husband's injuries. The post-mortem was carried out by Mr Boodle who found that the liver had been crushed, leading to a fatal haemorrhage.

In summing up, the Coroner said that there was no question as to the cause of death. After hearing all of the evidence presented, it was perfectly clear that it had occurred entirely through the action of the deceased getting into the van in the foolish way that he did, by which, in all probability, had frightened the animal. The Jury, without any hesitation, returned a verdict in accordance with the medical testimony.

Heydon Duke II was subsequently sold to a local butcher and slaughtered.

CHAPTER 10

A Shocking Case of Burning
1886

*Her entire body was covered in burns with not
a patch of skin... having escaped destruction*

One of the most distressing cases of accidental death to come before the Colchester Coroner's Court in the nineteenth century was that concerning the terrible burning of a twenty-year-old domestic servant named Ellen Ashby. Ellen was the daughter of Samuel and Harriet Ashby of Maidenburgh Street and at the time of the accident was in the employ of Mr Richard Ives, chief clerk at the Essex and Suffolk Fire Office, who lived with his wife, Alice, in private accommodation adjoining the building. Ellen had worked for the couple for almost two years before her position was so tragically terminated on the evening of Monday, 22 February 1886.

In the hours leading up to the accident Ellen's day would have been filled with the usual tasks associated with the duties of a general housemaid. Beginning at perhaps six-thirty in the morning she would have been busy attending to the needs of her employers and preparing breakfast, before moving on to general house cleaning, preparing lunch, making the beds, cleaning the brass and silverware and numerous other duties besides, until it would have been time to prepare and serve the evening meal. Only then would Ellen have found a little spare time for herself and, perhaps, a few moments to relax in front of a warm fire. She may have even dozed off for a few minutes and not have been aware that a small cinder, or piece of coal, had fallen from the fire. It is something which most of us who have memories of a traditional coal fire can easily relate to – an annoying yet commonplace problem which at worst could lead to a hole in the hearth rug or carpet. But on this occasion the cinder, or spark, which flew out from the fire landed somewhere on Ellen's clothing, with devastating consequences.

The first that Ellen realised that something was amiss was when she detected a faint smell of burning. For a moment or two she took little notice of the matter, but then was shocked into action when her dress suddenly burst into flames. In a state of sheer panic she rushed up and downstairs screaming for help. Within seconds of hearing her screams Mr Ives and his wife had rushed from their sitting room and found the poor girl standing outside the drawing room door enveloped in flames from head to foot. Meanwhile outside the building in the High Street several passers by had also become aware of the commotion within the building including Mr John Pollard, a cab driver, who happened to be passing the Fire Office at the time. After seeing Ellen, with her clothes in flames, running up the stairs towards Mr Ives's private apartments, he rushed to give assistance, intending that he could perhaps throw his rug over her, but to his frustration he found that the door to the

Colchester High Street, looking west, about 1886. On the right of the picture can be seen part of the Victorian Town Hall, whilst further along is the newly refurbished Cups Hotel. Note, also, the couple in the cart who have stopped to share a few moments with a passing pedestrian - something not possible in our modern traffic congested streets. Jess Jephcott

premises had slammed shut and would not open. He then saw
Mr Henry Laver (surgeon and Mayor of Colchester) passing
the building and ran over to tell him what had happened.
Meanwhile, two young men had managed to get the door open
and had rushed inside where they attempted to douse the
flames by throwing some water over the girl's burning body.

Inside the house, after rushing to his house servant's aid, Mr
Ives immediately threw her to the floor and began covering her
body with rugs, coats and any other material which was to
hand in a desperate attempt to put out the flames. In doing so
he suffered serious burns to his hands which were to take
several weeks to heal. Within a short space of time further help
had arrived in the form of several policemen, and Mr Henry
Laver who immediately took command of the situation. By this
time the poor girl's clothing had been almost completely burnt
off, with the exception of the bands of her petticoat and parts
of her sleeves and stockings. Her entire body was covered in
burns with not a patch of skin the size of a man's hand having
escaped destruction. Mr Laver did all he could to alleviate the
poor girl's sufferings, but could see that it was a pretty hopeless
case. At length a stretcher was brought to the house and she
was carried off to the hospital where the House Surgeon, Mr
B H Nicholson, did what he could for her. Through all of this
Ellen had remained perfectly conscious and was able to relate
a little about what had happened to her. However, such were
the extent of her injuries that she died a few hours later at half
past ten in the evening.

An inquest into the cause of her death was held at the Essex
and Colchester Hospital on the following Wednesday before
Mr Adolphus Church, the Borough Coroner. In detailing the
facts of the proceedings to the Jury, Mr Church said that it was
one of the most painful cases he had had to investigate, adding
that during all of his time in office, including when he assisted
his father, he could not recollect a case where a person had
been burnt in this way. The Jury then went to view the victim's
body, which presented a truly shocking appearance.

The first witness called to give evidence was Selina Ashby,
the deceased's sister-in-law, and who had been given the
painful task of identifying her body. She said that she had been

to see her sister-in-law at about a quarter to eight on the evening of her death, and had asked her how the accident had occurred. The deceased had told her that she had been sitting by the fire when a cinder fell out and set her dress alight. She said that she screamed for help but could not make anyone hear, as her master and mistress were upstairs having their tea with both the doors shut.

Mrs Alice Ives was the next witness called and told the court how she and her husband had been sitting in their living room when they had been startled by the sound of screaming:

My husband and I live in an apartment on the upper floor of the Essex and Suffolk Fire Office. The deceased had been in our employ for about two years and was a well conducted person. At about five o'clock on Monday evening my husband and I were having tea in a room on a floor above the kitchen. The tea had been served by the deceased who had then returned to the kitchen. A little while later we thought that we heard a noise and imagined that it might be someone coming up the stairs - and then we heard a scream. We both rushed downstairs and saw the deceased standing on a mat near the drawing room door enveloped in flames. She was screaming. My husband threw her down and put all the mats and coats he could lay his hands on over her.

The CORONER: *Your husband must have had great difficulty in getting hold of her?*
Answer: *Yes, it was that which caused the burns. He threw all the rugs and coats that he could find over her, and then Mr Laver came in. There were also two men there who threw some water on her.*

Mr Laver then told the court of his involvement in the incident:

At about a quarter past five on Monday afternoon I was passing the Fire Office, when Mr Pollard, a cabman, came up to me and said, 'A girl just came out of Mr Ives's door in flames, screamed 'Fire!' and then ran back in again.' I went in

Colchester High Street, looking east, in 1901. The Fire Office building on the left is where Ellen Ashby suffered her fatal burns. Note the horse-drawn cabs lined up in front of the building, and further along the street the scaffolding in place for the new Town Hall. Author's collection

as soon as I could get the door open, and found the deceased lying against the drawing room door as described, with two men, who had just preceded me, putting some water on her. I assisted in removing the burning clothes, and did what I could for her. I then sent down to the Police Station for a stretcher, and had her removed to the Hospital. As soon as I had got her into bed at the Hospital, I asked her how it had occurred. She told me that a coal had 'popped' out of the fire as she was sitting near it. She then noticed a slight scent of burning, of which she took no heed for a time, until her dress began to blaze. She then ran downstairs in fright, screaming for help, and her master and mistress then came to her assistance. I asked whether there was anyone there with her and she told me she was alone. I saw her afterwards and was present when she died about ten o'clock the same evening. The whole surface of her skin was more extensively burnt than I have ever seen before. She could not tell me whether the coal had fell on her dress or her underclothing, although if the dress had been made of non-inflammable material, it would not have burnt.

The CORONER: *Do you know for a fact that such material is procurable for dresses?*

Answer: *Dresses and everything may be dipped and made non-inflammable, and without any inconvenience in any way.*

A JUROR: *Would it not be well for the Jury to recommend that women's dresses be made of non-inflammable material?*

Answer: *It is not simply a material. It is a salt – tungstate of soda – which can be put with dresses, calicoes, and other things when they are washed. It renders them absolutely non-inflammable, and they cannot blaze. It does not interfere with the starching or the glossing iron, or anything.*

The Coroner then recalled a recent case where the ball dresses of two young ladies had caught fire in a similar fashion resulting in them both being badly burnt and dying from their injuries. He concluded that cooks and servants, and others who have to work near to fires, were at much greater risk and should be protected in this way. In conclusion, Mr Laver stated that the cause of death had been the result of shock to the system, caused by burns. The Jury then returned a verdict of Death from Accidental Burning and the enquiry was terminated.

By way of a brief postscript to this terrible case, it may be of interest to learn that something in the order of 200 clothing fire deaths are still being reported annually in the UK. For the most part they involve people in the over sixty-five age group with matches, cigarette lighters, candles and open fires being the main sources of ignition.

CHAPTER 11

Drowning at Middle Mill
1887

*Joshua...began crying for help, shouting
that he couldn't swim.*

One of the worst accident blackspots facing drivers in Colchester during the horse-drawn era was the short stretch of road which crossed the River Colne near Middle Mill. For it was here that the road led right down into the water and was a popular rendezvous with drivers of all kinds of carts and wagons as they broke their journeys across town to refresh and water their horses. All they had to do was drive down into the river, water their horse, and then drive out again – well at least that was the theory. Unfortunately, things did not always go according to plan with the result that some drivers would find themselves in difficulty as they mistakenly ventured into deep water – occasionally with disastrous results. The main cause of worry was the fact that although the riverbed was fairly shallow where one entered the water, as you moved closer to where the mill floodgates were located there were one or two deep holes which were apparently between sixteen and eighteen feet deep – obviously something which needed to be avoided at all costs.

Extraordinary Casualty at Colchester

A MAN AND A HORSE DROWNED.

RECOVERY OF THE BODIES.

EXCITING AND PAINFUL SCENES.

A few minutes after twelve o'clock yesterday (Friday) an accident of an extraordinary, though not unprecedented, character occurred at Middle Mill, Colchester, by which a man named Joshua Charles Dunt, and a horse he was driving, were drowned. The deceased man was 21 years of age in February last, and was the only son of Joshua Dunt, tailor, Priory Street, with whom he has been residing.

A contemporary newspaper report of the tragic drowning.
Author's collection

One of the worst cases of drowning at this location, however, was that which took place on Friday, 8 July 1887. It involved a twenty-one-year-old man named Joshua Charles Dunt, who lived with his father, a local tailor, in Priory Street. Joshua had recently completed an engineering apprenticeship with Messrs Davey, Paxman and Co, and whilst waiting for a vacancy to occur with that firm he had been doing some odd jobs for a Mr Howard, a local Carter (light haulage work), in Culver Street. On the day of the accident Joshua had been instructed to take one of his master's horses and a tumbril (a small two-wheeled cart) to deliver some materials from the site of the new Wesleyan School, which was being built in Culver Street, down to the Great Eastern Railway Company's new laundry works near North Station. When he had completed the delivery and was making his way back to town, along St Peter's Street, he decided to drive his cart into the pond at Middle Mill in order to water his horse. The route through town via St Peter's Street and Maidenburgh Street, rather than simply going up North Hill, was much preferred by the town's horse drivers as Maidenburgh Street, although of a similar incline to North Hill, proved much easier for the horses to negotiate.

But no sooner had Joshua driven his cart into the stream and made a start to come out again, he found himself in serious difficulty. After entering the water he appears to have driven round to his left before beginning the turn back towards the bank, but not being acquainted with the dangers of the spot, he had directed his horse straight into one of the deep floodgate holes. As soon as the horse lost its footing it immediately started to swim towards the bank, and in doing so pulled the cart, and Joshua, into the hole as well. Joshua quickly found himself up to his shoulders in water and began crying out for help, shouting that he couldn't swim. At this stage had he simply kept his nerve and held on tight to the cart his horse would probably have saved him by swimming its way out of difficulty and dragging the cart behind him. But understandably Joshua panicked and made the mistake of pulling back on the horse's reins resulting in both horse and man floundering dangerously above the seventeen feet deep hole.

The River Colne at Middle Mill was a popular place for watering and refreshing one's horses. c.1930. Author's collection

Meanwhile, the owner of the nearby mill, Mr Ezekial Chopping, his son William, and several other mill workers having been alerted to the commotion, rushed to the scene to see what assistance they could give to the desperate young man. When they arrived at the water's edge all they could see were the feet of the horse kicking wildly in the air – its body being submerged – and young Joshua clinging desperately to the cart with just his head and shoulders above water. Mr Chopping at once procured some ropes and, after grabbing hold of a small lifebuoy, his son William bravely swam out to the spot to render help. However, just before he got there, Joshua's head sank below the surface and he was not seen again. At the same time the horse entirely disappeared and it seemed likely that Joshua's body must somehow have been caught up in the horse's reins, and as the horse sank he was dragged down to his death.

Mr Chopping (junior) swam backwards and forwards to the spot several times but no trace could be seen either of Joshua, the horse, or the cart. As news of the accident spread a large crowd assembled in the vicinity of the mill and, of course, the

Middle Mill as it appeared in the 1920s.
Jess Jephcott

police had also been notified. After some considerable time had elapsed a small boat, which had been found moored a short distance away, was finally lifted out of the river and launched into the pond where Police Constable Alexander and a few other men, armed with grappling hooks, were preparing to row out into the stream to search for the body. But just as they were about to commence their search Joshua's body suddenly popped to the surface about twenty yards from the riverbank, accompanied by one of the horse's feet. This, of course, caused considerable excitement among the many hundreds of people who were by now crowded along the banks of the river. The boat was immediately rowed out to the spot and by means of a hook one of the dead man's arms was secured, and after a cord had been tied to his wrist an attempt was made to pull the body away. This proved to be a difficult operation as the body was found to be entangled in the horse's harness, but it was finally released and slowly floated to the surface. Once again there were gasps of horror, and many tears, from the watching crowd, particularly when Joshua's white upturned face came into view. He was found to be still clutching his whip which could only be prised from his hand with great difficulty. The body was then towed gently to the side of the pond before being placed upon a hurdle and then carried to a shed attached to the nearby *Oddfellows' Arms*.

During an attempt to extricate the horse (a valuable bay worth about £30) a man named James Graham, an employee of the nearby mineral water premises in Factory Lane, and in charge of a van and pair of horses, had decided to lend a hand and had driven his horses down into the river to where the rescue operation was taking place. Apparently, the dead horse at this time was lying on its back with just its head and feet protruding from the water, with the cart still attached to its

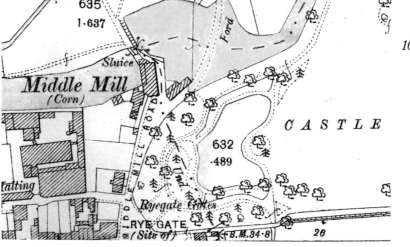

Part of a nineteenth century Ordnance Survey map showing the site of Middle Mill and the old ford across the river. Author's collection

harness. Graham allowed the party of rescuers to attach a rope to his van whilst the other end was tied to the submerged cart. He had told them to fasten the rope to the axle of the van, but instead they had tied it to the scroll iron of the spring. The result of this action was that as soon as Graham urged his horses forward towards the shore the van completely capsized depositing hundreds of mineral water bottles into the river. Some floated, some sank, others were smashed, all to the great excitement of the crowd. However, despite having suffered a bit of a drenching, Graham was unhurt and quickly set off in pursuit of his horses which had succeeded in breaking away from the capsized van in the direction of the bank.

The official inquest into the cause of the man's death was held later on the same day at the *Oddfellows' Arms* where the body had earlier been laid to rest. The first witness called was the deceased's father (Joshua Dunt) who stated that the last time he had seen his son alive was on Thursday night at ten o'clock, when he had told him that he was going to do some work for Mr Howard the following day. One of the main eyewitnesses to the event, however, was a man named Alfred Wood, a horse clipper, who resided in Angle Lane (West Stockwell Street):

> *I was walking in the meadow near the mill at about 12.30 when I saw the deceased driving a horse attached to a light tumbril. He then drove it into the water apparently for the purpose of refreshing his horse. The horse then went into a hole*

The Odd Fellows' Arms *on the corner of St Peter's Street and Maidenburgh Street where the body of Joshua Dunt was laid out after being retrieved from the river. c.1880s.* Jess Jephcott

in the mill pond, and the deceased pulled the horse on its back, and he sank down with the horse and cart. I told him to jump out, but he said that he couldn't swim. Mr Chopping then got undressed and swam over the spot with a lifebuoy, but he said that he couldn't see him. The police then came down and after getting a boat managed to get the deceased out of the water. He had then been in the water between twenty minutes and half an hour. I would say that about three or four minutes had elapsed from the time that the deceased first called out for help up to the time that he sank. And after sinking down he never came up again.

Mr William Chopping then told the court that he had been working in the mill about twelve-thirty, when he had heard someone call out that a horse was drowning. He then ran to the spot where he heard the deceased cry out, 'I can't swim!' He then undressed and swam out to the spot where he had first seen him, but by the time he had got there he had gone down.

At the conclusion of the proceedings, the Jury returned a

The River Colne as it appears today at the same site. The former mill stood near the centre of the picture and was demolished in the 1950s. The Author

verdict of 'Accidental Drowning.' The Foreman added that he and the others of the Jury had visited the scene of the accident and were unanimously of the opinion that the west side of the roadway across the river should be protected by chains or piles, or at least something that would indicate where the danger was. He finished by saying that he himself had seen an elephant go into the water there, with nothing to be seen but its trunk.

CHAPTER 12

Tragedy at Wakes Colne
1888

*...he knelt on top of her and, despite her pleas for mercy,
ruthlessly drew his knife across her throat...*

One of the most distressing cases of murder investigated in the 1880s was that concerning the death of twenty-one-year-old Annie Sargeant, the mother of a six month old baby girl, who was killed by her husband George at Wakes Colne in July 1888. This was a classic case of domestic violence which had spiralled out of control, resulting in the death of both parents, and heartbreak to the families concerned. Unfortunately, domestic rows leading to violence were accepted as normal behaviour in many Victorian homes, particularly those of the poorer classes where the choice was often one of either feeding the family, or providing drink for the husband. Of course the husband would still expect to have his dinner on the table when he arrived home after a heavy drinking session, and many a desperate wife was forced to either sell or pawn what few possessions they had in order to try and keep the peace.

George and Annie Sargeant were married on 11 April 1887 and in the following January their joy must have seemed complete with the birth of their baby daughter Laura. However, the honeymoon period was to be short-lived and within a few months their marriage was on the rocks. George was known locally as a bit of lout with a drink problem, and one who wouldn't think twice about blowing all of his earnings in the local pub. At the time of the killing he was about thirty years of age and had spent a number of years serving with the Essex Regiment in India. After being discharged from the army, he had got a job as a Fettler (repair and maintenance) on the Great Eastern Railway, although shortly before the incident in question he had been dismissed for misconduct.

The trouble with the couple's marriage came to an abrupt

Lane Farm, Wakes Colne where Annie Sargeant was brutally murdered by her husband. The murder took place in the ground floor room to the left of the front entrance door. And on the day following the murder the Coroner's inquest was held in the very same room. Author's collection

head one day towards the end of June 1888 when George returned to their Copford home in a drunken state and set about smashing up the household furniture and crockery. His wife Annie and her mother (Mrs Mary Ann Punt), who were home at the time, were both absolutely terrified, and following his violent outburst he forced the two women from the building by deliberately exploding a fog-signal flare in the fireplace. His wife had finally reached the end of her tether and clutching her baby daughter and a handful of possessions, she left the house to go and live with her parents at Lane Farm, Wakes Colne.

Once he had sobered up, George repeatedly tried to get his wife to change her mind and about three weeks later, on Tuesday, 17 July, he went over to Wakes Colne in a last ditch attempt to persuade his wife to come home. When he arrived at the house he went straight through to the front sitting room and sat in a chair next to his wife. Mrs Punt, and her other daughter Emily, remained in one of the rooms at the back of the house, but were suddenly alarmed by loud screaming and rushed into the room where they had left Annie. They found Annie lying on the floor supporting a nasty stab wound to the side of her head. After getting to her feet she managed to make her escape and ran into the adjoining room, whilst her mother bravely grabbed hold of her son-in-law, despite him still brandishing the knife, but was quickly thrown down as he pursued his wife into the other room. After catching up with her he knelt on top of her and, despite her pleas for mercy, ruthlessly drew his knife across her throat, nearly severing her head in the process. He then kicked and stamped on her head several times before running from the building.

Outside the house, a number of people had been alerted to the commotion including a farm worker named William Davey who managed to trail Sargeant across a couple of fields before persuading him to give himself up. Both men then made their way back along a footpath towards the railway station where they waited for the police to arrive. After being cautioned and taken into custody by Police Constable Wade, Sargeant was taken off to Halstead. The prisoner

A contemporary newspaper drawing of the prisoner, George Sargeant. Author's collection

showed little emotion or remorse for what he had done other than to remark: 'I hope that she will go to Heaven, for I know I shall go to Hell.'

The Coroner's inquest was held the following day at Lane Farm, in the very same room where the murder had been committed. The deceased's body was lying in the adjoining room and the atmosphere was extremely tense. The prisoner was brought into the room in handcuffs, which were later removed when the proceedings got under way. Sargeant was

A view of the impressive looking railway viaduct which crosses the Colne valley at Chappel and Wakes Colne. 2005 The Author

described as being six feet tall with a robust figure and strong features. His hair was thick and curly and hung over his face giving him something of an Italian appearance. He sat throughout most of the proceedings with his head buried in his hands, only speaking when spoken to, and only then to say 'No Sir,' to the Coroner when asked if he had anything to say after each of the witnesses had given their evidence.

The first witness called to give evidence was the victim's younger sister Emily Punt, who said that she saw the prisoner come into the house at nine-thirty the previous morning:

I was standing in the kitchen when he came in and pushed past me to go into the sitting room, I went in and saw him sitting beside Annie - he was talking to her, but they were not arguing. A little while later I was in the kitchen when I heard her call out, 'Oh mother, mother!'. This was just before ten o'clock and I ran in to see what was the matter. She had got her hand up and was saying, 'Oh don't, George, don't!' . I then ran out and called Mrs Bull next door. When I came back Annie was on the floor and George had hold of her hair. I took hold of her hand and called, 'Annie, Annie', but she was dead – she couldn't answer me.

At this stage of the proceedings the witness was overcome with grief, but after a short while was able to continue with her evidence:

There was a lot of blood on the floor and George was kneeling against her all the time. He then kicked her on the face before leaving the room and going out into the cow-yard. He stood by the railings for a few minutes, but when he saw my father coming he went off across the fields through the stackyard.

Having completed her evidence with as much composure as could be expected, the pressure of the occasion got too much for her and she became quite hysterical as she went to leave the room. Apparently, the nearest way out of the room would involve her passing close to the prisoner but she cried out that she could not pass him, and was taken out by another exit.

The next witness to be called was the victim's mother, Mrs Mary Ann Punt, who went into some detail concerning the months and weeks which led up to the killing. In describing the events of the occasion three weeks earlier when the prisoner had returned home drunk and destroyed the furniture, she recalled how she had to shield her daughter from her husband's attempts to cause her injury:

> *He was holding his hand up as though to strike her, but I stood between them with the baby in my arms and prevented it. I told him, no blows and Annie then ran out into the yard. He then locked the doors of the house and we didn't go inside anymore.*

She then explained that on the day before the murder she and her daughter had been walking along the road from Colne station about six o'clock in the evening when they met the prisoner in the road leading to Lane Farm. He came up to Annie and asked her to go back and live with him, she said:

> *Annie replied, 'How can I, when you have broken up all the things in the house.' She told him that if he would go to work and earn some money to replace the things that he'd broken, and make things comfortable for her, then she would go back. She said that she could not go back and live the life that she'd had before. We stood in the road and talked with him until nearly eight o'clock.*

Moving on to the events of the following day, she described in graphic terms how the prisoner had attacked her daughter and ended her life:

> *About 9.30 yesterday morning he came to my house again. He walked in the kitchen door and went through to the sitting room where Annie was sitting. About a quarter of an hour later I heard my daughter scream and call out, 'Oh mother, oh mother.' I rushed into the room and saw her running round the table with a gash in her neck. She was saying, 'Don't George,*

don't', and he said, 'I will do it, I will.' I managed to get hold
of his left hand from across the table, but he went down on his
knees and put the knife into her again. I can't say whether it
was into her neck or her face. He then pushed me away and I
fell into the corner of the room. He then got his right foot and
struck his heel into poor Annie's head as she lay on the floor.
When I got up he followed me into the little room – my room,
and said, 'Mother, kiss me, kiss me.' After that he walked out
through the kitchen and into the cow-yard.

The only other person to have witnessed the murder was
Martha Bull, the daughter of Mrs Punt's neighbour. Miss Bull
was a youngish looking woman who was neatly dressed in
mourning apparel. She told the court that at about 10 o'clock
on the day of the murder she was upstairs in her house when
she heard screams coming from next door:

I rushed down and went through Mrs Punt's kitchen into the
sitting room. I saw Sargeant come from Mrs Punt and he went
and knelt down beside Annie. She was lying on the floor with
her head under the table and I saw him draw his right hand
across her throat. I didn't see anything in his hand, but she just
lay there in a pool of blood. I then rushed out and called my
father.

The next witness called to give evidence was William Davey,
the farm worker, who had apprehended the prisoner shortly
after the murder. The Coroner began by asking him if he could
clarify how his name was spelt, but the witness, not knowing
himself, simply replied, 'I'm sure I don't know hardly,' and
with that the Coroner asked him to proceed with his evidence.
He then went on to explain the circumstances of how he had
come across the prisoner on the previous morning shortly after
he had fled from the house:

Yesterday morning, between ten and eleven, I saw the prisoner
on the railway bridge near Old House Farm. I was walking
across the field when I saw him walking along the road. I had

*earlier been called away from my work and was aware of what
had happened. I followed him to where he stopped to sit on the
grass beneath a tree and then went up to him and said that I
knew he had cut his wife's throat and that I wanted him to
come with me. He said to me, 'I've done it', and I took him to
the corner of the road as you go up to the station and we sat
and waited for the constable to come along.*

After hearing further evidence from the police and the surgeon
who performed the post-mortem, the Coroner drew the
proceedings to a close and said that all that now remained was
for the Jury to return their verdict. In his summary of the
proceedings he explained that the witnesses had all given a
clear account of what had happened and that the Jury should
have no trouble in deciding that the deceased woman was
murdered by the prisoner, George Sargeant. The Jury at once
returned a verdict of Wilful Murder against George Sargeant,
who was then   handed over to the police and taken in
handcuffs to Colchester. When in the custody of the police the
prisoner apparently broke down and burst out crying, saying
that he wanted to see his wife before she was buried and that
how he had always loved her very much. After arriving at
Colchester County Police Station, however, his demeanour
returned to one of quiet apathy, and he appeared to be totally
resigned to his fate. Even so, he maintained a healthy appetite
during his period of incarceration, eating three times as much
as an ordinary man.

The next day, Thursday, 19 July 1888, the prisoner was on
the move once again, this time appearing before the Colchester
Magistrates where he was formally charged with his wife's
murder. The prisoner was due to appear in court at eleven
o'clock in the morning and by ten-thirty a large crowd had
gathered outside to witness his arrival. They also watched the
arrival of the dead woman's parents who were in a very
distressed condition and had to be helped up the steps of the
building by a policeman. And then, at about ten minutes to
eleven, the prisoner was driven up to the Town Hall in a cart
from the County Police Station on Ipswich Road. Within a few
minutes he had been ushered into the court and was standing

The old convict gaol at Chelmsford. c.1810. Author's collection

in the dock guarded by two policemen. He had a dejected look about him and appeared rather thin about the face, although his hair was neat and tidy suggesting that he may have had it trimmed. The evidence given was much the same as that presented to the Coroner and at the end of the proceedings the prisoner was formerly committed for trial at the Summer Assize, which was due to commence on the following Monday. The prisoner was then taken from the court in a cab to the railway station and from there to Springfield Gaol at Chelmsford to await his trial.

The trial took place on Wednesday, 25 July at the Shire Hall, Chelmsford. The prisoner arrived in an ordinary prison van just before ten-thirty in the morning, and shortly thereafter His Lordship, Mr Baron Pollock, entered the courtroom and took his seat. The prisoner was then arraigned and when asked by the Clerk how he pleaded to the charge of murder, he replied in a low but clear voice: 'Guilty Sir.' The prisoner appeared composed and showed no sign of nerves. When asked if he had anything to say before sentence was passed upon him, he replied in a firm voice: 'No Sir.' His Lordship then placed the black cap upon his head and directed the following words to the prisoner:

George Sargeant, you have pleaded guilty to the wilful murder of your own wife, a woman who by all laws, human and divine, you were bound to protect and to comfort. As you must be well aware, there is but one sentence which the law awards for a crime of this kind, and that sentence it is my duty now to pass. When I have passed that sentence my duty ends and I cannot hold out to you any hope that any other event can take place other than that this sentence will be carried out. I can only hope that the same mind and spirit which have led you to confess before a human tribunal the guilt of that terrible offence will lead you to turn for pardon and repentance to God, who alone can give it. You will have, during the short time which is given you in this life, the kind comfort and assistance of those who will be able to help you in turning to Him in this time of your need. The sentence of this court is that you be taken from hence to the place from whence you came, and from thence to a place of execution, and that you be there hanged by the neck until you shall be dead, and that your body be afterwards buried within the precincts of the prison in which you shall have been last confined after your conviction, and may the Lord have mercy on your soul.

As the sentence was being read out a deadly hush pervaded the courtroom. All eyes were now on the prisoner who remained perfectly calm and composed throughout, showing no sign of stress or fear. After the Judge had concluded reading the final words of condemnation, the prisoner was taken from the court and returned to Springfield Gaol to await his execution, which was planned for three weeks time on Wednesday, 15 August at eight o'clock in the morning (this three week period of grace was the usual time given to the condemned person as a time for repentance and for attending to affairs of the soul). Over the next few weeks George Sargeant found plenty of time to reflect on his situation, and is said to have become very penitent and dejected. He spent much of his time in the prison chapel where he tried to make his peace with God and come to terms with his situation. He was also visited by one of his old army friends, which was a great comfort to him, and by his parents and married brother, William, who made the journey to Chelmsford by train from their homes in Suffolk. In fact, the prisoner's mother had broken her journey to the prison at Wakes Colne station where she had visited the home of Mr and Mrs Punt where the murder had been committed. The reason for the visit was to take possession of her son's baby daughter as it had been his desire that she be brought up by his own parents. This was obviously a very distressing time for the deceased's family who eventually were forced to hand the child over.

Meanwhile, the prisoner's father and brother continued their journey to Chelmsford where they spent about an hour or so with the condemned man. The father later stated that he found his son much more composed than he had expected, although he said he was concerned as to what was to become of his little child. He said he also wanted to know if it was true that the newspapers were saying that he had broken up all his furniture, an act which he vehemently denied. The father also stated that he would never forget the moment when he had to say goodbye to his son. He admitted that at the time he could say very little but had since frequently broken down and burst into tears. Just two days before his execution the prisoner had another visit from his mother who was accompanied by his sister, Sarah, and his baby child. They had arrived at Chelmsford Railway Station at eleven-thirty that morning and were driven to the gaol in a horse-drawn omnibus. The meeting lasted for about half an hour and was also attended by the prison Chaplain, who had previously warned the visitors against saying anything that might distract the condemned man's thoughts from the all too certain future that he was now hastening towards. As soon as he saw his 'darling daughter, Laura,' as he called her, he took her into his arms and nursed her until the final goodbyes had to be said. At the time of the final parting he made his mother promise to go and put some flowers on his wife's grave, and said that he hoped that he would soon be meeting her in a better place.

The following day – on the eve of his execution – he wrote a final letter to his mother and father which is here reproduced in full:

NB: As the prisoner himself could not read or write, the letter was probably written for him by the prison Chaplain, for in a previous letter sent to his mother, he speaks of the 'clergyman' reading her letter to him.

H. M. Gaol, Chelmsford. Aug. 14 1888

My dear Mother and Father, - I now write to you for the last time, to send you and all my brothers and sisters my fondest love, to my brother Bill and his wife, to their two dear little children; kiss the little ones for me. I don't forget Charlie in India. Also love to my sister Laura, who I should have liked to see. I hope my sister Sarah is better; and, above all, kiss my little baby for me. I thought of her last night lying on my bed. I think it ought to have a little ring to put in its mouth now she is cutting her teeth, it would comfort her a little. Love to all my aunts and uncles, and all friends that I know, and all who have kindly thought and prayed for me. I must not forget old John Peachy and his wife, with whom I worked at Chappel. Give my respects to Mr Hollingsworth, to Mr Cracknell, and all the mates I worked with. James Eve and his wife at Aldham, Ford Street, and all that know me round about. Mr Crosby and his wife and child, and Mr Grimwade and his wife. Dear mother and father, do not fret for me. I hope to meet you some day in heaven. Do not forget what I told you about the flowers on my wife's grave. I have prayed that I may meet her in heaven through the loving mercy of my God and Saviour, for I have deeply repented of my wrong, which I heartily wish had never happened, but I then felt that I had great cause, and little thought of what I was doing. Don't forget to thank Mr Patten (with my love, for he sent his to me) at Chappel Station for the kindness he and others have shown to you and my dear child. I must say while I have been here that I have been kindly treated, and have had all I wanted – everything I have wished I have had. In my prayers and services I have had every help, and I do feel that they have been blest to me, as I now feel kindly towards everyone. May God help you and me to bear up under this great trial, and in

His mercy may He bless us all now and for ever. Again I send my love to my baby. I hope you will be spared to look to her, and that God may keep you both, for it is no fault of yours that this has happened. I now fully forgive the wrongs I felt done to me, and I hope all is forgiven to me. Now I must give up this earth. I hope to go to a happier place – that to a poor sinner. Heaven's gate may be open through the blood shed for me by my Saviour, and I hope all will have a share in this great salvation, which I have now learnt is the gift of God, and not what anyone can deserve. My love to all again, and may God help us. Always think of me, dear mother and father.

Your affectionate and loving son,
George Sargeant

Following the court's decision for George Sargeant to suffer the death penalty, the prison authorities wasted little time in preparing for the event to take place. Arrangements had to be made for the erection of the scaffold and for ensuring that it was operating correctly, and also to secure the services of The Hangman. The man chosen for this task was James Berry from Bradford who later became the first British executioner to write about his work *(My Experiences as an Executioner)*. Mr Berry arrived in Chelmsford by train at six-twenty on the evening before the execution. He was wearing a check suit and black hat, and in his hand he carried a black bag which contained his ropes, straps and other paraphernalia pursuant to his trade. He was at once driven to the gaol where he set about testing the scaffold and the drop with a dummy of similar size and weight to the prisoner. Satisfied that everything was in order he retired for the night in accommodation provided within the prison.

The following morning, the prisoner was up and dressed soon after six-thirty, after having had a reasonable night's sleep. He then enjoyed a good breakfast of two eggs, bread and butter and tea, although understandably appeared quite depressed. At seven forty-five the Chapel bell announced that the time of his execution was drawing near. A few minutes later Mr Berry

Professional hangman James Berry, of Bradford, was given the task of despatching George Sargeant on the gallows at Springfield Gaol.
Anonymous - James Berry's autobiography

entered the condemned man's cell where he proceeded to pinion his arms at his sides before leading him off towards the scaffold in a mournful procession which included the Governor of the prison and the Chaplain. The prisoner appeared to be in good health, despite being unshaven, and walked firmly, without assistance, to the scaffold where he shook hands with the warders and Mr Berry. By this time, of course, all executions were carried out in private, except for a small representation from the press which on this occasion extended to eight. As the prisoner stood beneath the rope his lips were seen to quiver a little but his face was then quickly engulfed beneath the white hood which was placed over his head. Seconds later, Berry drew the bolt and Sargeant's body dropped several feet until it was hanging in mid-air, slightly twitching but nothing that could be described as a struggle. And then his body became still as life was extinguished.

For the small group of people who had assembled outside the gaol, the appearance of the black flag being hoisted on its pole confirmed that the deed had been carried out. About an hour later the body was removed from the scaffold and was examined by the prison surgeon who confirmed that death had been caused by the fracture of the neck and windpipe. The assembled Jury were satisfied that the sentence of death had been carried out in accordance with the law, and the body was then taken away and buried in a small plot which had been prepared in the prison grounds. And thus brought to an end this tragic sequence of events which had so cruelly robbed a young child of both its mother and father. For the surviving relatives, however, the misery must have lingered on, perhaps never to have been forgotten as they lived out their lives under the shadow of this terrible crime.

CHAPTER **13**

A Moment of Madness
1891

The Colchester Tragedy

If only it were possible to look into the future and to see the heartache and distress that is caused by mindless acts of violence, particularly those leading to the loss of life. Surely then those responsible for committing such crimes would have done things differently. Sadly, of course, we can only claim to be wise after the event and countless lives have been lost or ruined by these moments of madness. The case which we are now going to examine fits neatly into this scenario. It was described in the press at the time as 'The Colchester Tragedy' and was indeed the result of a few moments of madness on the part of Thomas Sadler who brutally murdered his love rival, William Wass. Not only was the life of an innocent man so cruelly taken from him, but his five children were robbed of their father, his wife of her husband and his mother of her son. Even the murderer's own

THE COLCHESTER TRAGEDY.

DEATH OF THE WOUNDED MAN.

WASS'S DYING STATEMENT.

About ten minutes to nine on Thursday morning William Wass, who, it will be remembered, was stabbed at his house in Bromley Road on Monday night, May 25, by Thomas William Sadler, of West Street, succumbed to his injuries in spite of the best medical attendance, and on Monday Sadler (who is now in Springfield Gaol) will be charged before the

A contemporary newspaper report recording William Wass's deathbed statement to the police. Author's collection

family were not immune to the fall-out of his actions, with his poor old father at his wits' end at the prospect of seeing his son face the hangman's noose.

The events which led up to the tragedy had all the hallmarks of a drama of betrayal and deceit. Thomas Sadler, a thirty-year-old former soldier, had been lodging with William Wass and his family for a number of years before suddenly leaving the house, in August 1890, following a quarrel with his landlord. It would seem that at some stage during his stay with the family he had taken advantage of the situation by making a play for William's wife, Eliza. The couple had started an affair which was probably the reason for the family bust up and which led to Sadler moving out. A few weeks later William's wife followed, taking with her the youngest of her five children – the other four she left at home with their father.

The errant couple then went and took lodgings in a house in West Street belonging to a Mrs Edith Johnson, who later told the police that she was a respectable woman and had assumed that the couple had been man and wife. For the next six months Mrs Wass saw nothing of her husband, or indeed any of her four older children. For her husband's part he had done his best to feed, clothe and maintain the children whilst struggling to hold down a physically demanding job as an agricultural labourer. But then one day in May 1891, and completely out of the blue, Mrs Wass was seized with a desire to see her children, and had asked Mrs Johnson (with whom she was lodging) if she would secretly collect the children from their school and bring them to her. The plan was put into operation and having collected the children from their school in Harwich Road she was in the process of walking them home when she was confronted by Mr Wass who immediately took charge of the children and turned them round.

When she arrived back at West Street empty handed and told Mrs Wass what had happened, Sadler went on to say, 'Never mind, I will see if I can fetch them for you.' He then changed his clothes, went out, but returned almost immediately saying that he had forgotten his knife (the weapon with which the murder was committed) and that he needed it to cut his tobacco with. This would have been about eleven o'clock in the morning. Where he spent the next few hours is not known, but at nine o'clock in the evening he turned up at William Wass's Bromley Road home.

When he knocked on the door Mr Wass was sitting at his table mending a bag, with his twelve-year-old son, Hector, by his side. When he went to open the door and saw that it was Sadler outside he quickly tried to close it again, but Sadler, being a younger and stronger man forced his way inside. 'You wouldn't let the children come to see their mother, would you?' he said. 'Where's the girl Florrie?' 'She is upstairs, in bed and asleep,' replied her father, who at the same time made his way to the door at the foot of the stairs in an attempt to bar access to the upper floor. At this point a struggle ensued between the two men and Wass was forced away from the door towards the table, where Sadler stabbed him in the side of the head, exclaiming, 'You are a dead man.' The injured man then managed to get away and ran, with blood pouring from his wound, to a neighbour's property to seek help. He was followed by Sadler who was shouting along the way that he hoped that he had killed him, and that is what he had intended. The police and medical assistance were immediately sent for and, while Sadler was taken into custody, the injured man's wounds were treated. At the time of the attack it was hoped that his injuries were not too severe and that he would make a full recovery, but the bleeding continued, and when a secondary haemorrhage occurred about a week later his condition deteriorated, leading to his death on Thursday, 4 June.

Previous to Wass's death, Sadler was brought before the Colchester Magistrates' Court where he was charged with attempted murder (a charge which was later changed to one of murder). As soon as the doors of the court had been thrown open there was a great rush from those eager to get inside, and long before the Justices had occupied their seats on the bench, every available space had been occupied. It was noted that among the spectators, the fair sex predominated, and that these lovers of the sensational were to be in for a treat when the court was to hear evidence from Dr Ryan concerning details of the victim's injuries. A great deal of evidence was presented by the prosecution, although Mr Wass, who was still clinging to life at this time, was too ill to attend. Once the preliminary evidence had been heard, the case was adjourned until the following week, when it was hoped that Mr Wass himself would be well enough to attend. However, on the following Tuesday, his condition began to deteriorate and he died just two days later, on Thursday morning. Throughout this period he had been confined to his bed whilst being regularly attended to by a team of doctors. His aged mother had also been in regular attendance at his bedside, as had several other men and women from the neighbourhood.

On the Friday morning an inquiry into the circumstances surrounding his death was held in the Town Hall before the Borough Coroner, Mr Adolphus Church. In opening the proceedings, the Coroner provided those present with a brief account of the case to date which had sadly led to the death of William Wass, a forty-four-year-old father of five. The Jury were then taken in two horse carriages to Bromley Road to view the body of the deceased.

When they had reassembled in court the first witness called to give evidence was Hector Wass, the twelve-year-son of the deceased who had been sitting with his father when the attack took place. He confirmed his name and age before telling the court that on 25 May, about nine in the evening, he was sitting in the lower room of his father's house when he heard a knock at the back door. When his father went to see who it was he said that Sadler came in and started arguing with his father:

> When Sadler entered the house he said, 'Bill – you would not let the children come to see their mother, would you?' He was very angry, but father did not reply and made for the stairs. Sadler then said, 'Where is the girl Florrie?' meaning my sister. He then got hold of father's arm and tried to pull him back, whereupon father said, 'Tom, don't tear my shirt', but he kept pulling father against the wall and was swearing at him. After that he took his knife and stabbed him. My father then ran out of the house and shouted for Mr Tatam, who lives next door. When he returned to the house with Mr Tatam, Sadler said that 'he would like to give father another dab', and then said, 'Bill, you're a dead man.'

The next person called was Mr Isaac Tatam, firewood merchant, who had rendered aid to the deceased immediately after the attack:

On the night named, about nine o'clock, I was sitting in my house when I heard the shout of 'Murder, Mr Tatam, pray come here.' I went to the door as quickly as possible and saw Mr Wass, who was standing just outside. Sadler was standing about two yards behind him. Mr Wass then rushed up and clung to me saying, 'He's done it.' I said, 'Done what?' And he replied, 'He's cut me; he's killed me I believe.' I then looked at Sadler and said, 'Tom, what have you done to him?' Sadler replied, 'I have done the _____, I hope I have killed him. I intended to.' He also said, 'And I give myself up to you to give me in charge.' I saw that Wass was bleeding badly from near his left ear and tied a handkerchief round the wound. My brother-in-law, Mr Hurrell, then came up and helped me take the deceased back to his home. Sadler followed us using very bad language. When we got him inside the house Sadler said, 'I have not done enough to him yet, I don't think. I should like to have another tap.' He had still got the knife in his hand at the time, and he said, 'I shan't be particular to any of you if you get in my way, I might as well have three or four of you now I am about it.' My brother-in-law then made for the fireplace and when Sadler caught sight of that he walked out. He went out in the yard and said, 'I am going to the Royal Oak (a nearby public house). Send for a _____Policeman and give me in charge. I shan't run away.' I followed him up the road and saw him go into the Royal Oak. Another man had gone for a policeman and I waited outside the Royal Oak until he came. I then saw Police-constable Alexander going towards the house and told him what had happened and that Sadler was inside the pub. Alexander then went inside the Royal Oak and took the knife out of Sadler's breast pocket. He then took him back to Mr Wass's house before charging him with attempting to murder Mr Wass and I then drove them to the Police Station.

The Former Royal Oak *public house, Parson's Heath, as it appeared in 1935.*
Jess Jephcott

Police Constable Charles Alexander, who is stationed at Parson's Heath, then told the court how he had heard about the disturbance on the night in question:

> *On the evening named, about 9.30 pm, I received information that a man had been stabbed in Bromley Road. I ran to the scene as hard as possible and when I got to the top of the road, I met the last witness, who told me where the prisoner was. I entered the Royal Oak and saw the prisoner in the tap-room. He was wearing a light coat and I could see blood stains on the collar. I said to him, 'What's this on your coat, Sadler?' He said, 'Blood, I'm the man that did the _____ deed, I've stabbed old Bill Wass, and I hope to _____ he's dead.' I then cautioned the prisoner in the usual way, and he said, 'I'm perfectly aware of what I am saying and what I have done.' I then took the prisoner down to the deceased's home and saw him sitting in a chair. His head was bound up with a towel and he appeared to be exhausted. His shirt, vest and trousers were covered with blood. I had a conversation with him and he told me that he thought he was wounded near the ear. The*

The junction with Harwich Road and Bromley Road in 1910. The picture was taken looking directly towards Bromley Road where just a few buildings can be observed in a decidedly rural setting. Today, this road provides access to the large modern Greenstead housing estate. Author's collection

prisoner, who was sitting nearby, said, 'Have I cut your _____ windpipe Bill. If I haven't I meant to.' Sadler then turned to me and said, 'Do you think the _____ will die? If you think he won't give me my _____ knife and I'll finish him off now.' I then handcuffed him and Mr Tatam drove us to the station.

At this stage in the proceedings Mr C E Denton, Assistant Magistrates' Clerk, told the court that as a consequence of information received from the police on Tuesday morning, concerning the health of the injured man, he had accompanied the Mayor and Mr Coombs (the Head Constable) along with several other police officers to the home of the deceased, where he had made the following deathbed statement:

On Monday night, a week ago, about nine o'clock, I was at home when I heard a knock at my door. I opened it and Tom Sadler came in. I knew him as he had been lodging with me until the latter part of last August. About six weeks before last

Christmas my wife left me and went to live with him. When he came into my house he said, 'You wouldn't let the children go and see their mother today.' I said, 'No, they shall not.' He said, 'Where is Flora?' I replied, 'She is in bed and asleep.' He again asked for her and asked me to fetch her down, as he wanted her. I told him again she was in bed and asleep. He then struck at me and the blow caught me just in front of my left ear. I felt the blood and ran out of the house and he came after me. When he struck me he said, 'You are a dead man.' I had not had any quarrel with him before. I had not seen him or my wife since she left me. I heard him say at Tatam's, to whose house I ran, 'If I haven't given him enough I should like to give him another one.' After I went back to my house, he said, in the presence of Alexander, 'Did I catch you in the windpipe Bill – I meant to do it.' My wound began to bleed again last night. I am very ill, too ill to say any more. I have made this statement fearing I shall die. I have no hope of recovering from the wound. My wound keeps bleeding and I believe I am dying.

Harwich Road, looking downhill towards Colchester town centre about two miles distant 1910. Author's collection

There was then some excitement in the court as the deceased's widow, Eliza Wass, took the stand. She appeared to be quite agitated by the whole process and made the following statement:

> *The deceased, who was my husband, was about forty-seven years of age. We had five children. The prisoner, Sadler, used to lodge with us, and did so for eleven years. He used to be on excellent terms with my husband and had no quarrel with him at home. After last harvest, about the month of August, Sadler left.*

The CORONER: *Why?*
Answer: *They had a quarrel.*
Question: *Did you leave your husband?*
Answer: *Yes.*
Question: *Where did you live?*
Answer: *In West Street.*
Question: *What became of Sadler?*
Answer: *He came to live with me, and has lived with me ever since.*
Question: *Did you bring any of your children away?*
Answer: *Yes, the youngest, and left the other four with my husband.*
Question: *On Monday morning was anything said to Sadler about the children?*
Answer: *Yes, I said to him, 'I should like to see my children.'*

[At this stage the witness was allowed to sit down.]

The CORONER: *What did Sadler say?*
Answer: *He said he would see if he could fetch them to me.*
Question: *And what else was said?*
Answer: *He did not say any more.*
Question: *What did Mrs Johnson say?*
Answer: *She said she got the children as far as Magdalen Church.*

[At this point the witness began to feel faint and she was handed a glass of water.]

The CORONER: *And what happened after that?*
Answer: *When the children got as far as Magdalen Church, my husband turned them back. Sadler then said that he would see if he could fetch them for me.*
Question: *Did Sadler seem annoyed?*
Answer: *No, sir.*
Question: *Did he seem angry?*
Answer: *No.*
Question: *When did Sadler leave?*
Answer: *About eleven, and I have not seen him since.*

A great deal of time was then given to hearing the evidence of no less than four doctors who had assisted in trying to stem the bleeding from the deceased's wound. The Coroner then summarised the day's proceedings before bringing the investigation to a close. He did not think that the Jury would have any difficulty in bringing a verdict of wilful murder, although he was glad to think that it would not be their verdict which would settle the case, as that responsibility would belong to a higher court. The Jury then retired for a short period to consider their verdict before returning to the court:

The CORONER: *Mr Foreman and gentlemen of the Jury, have you agreed upon your verdict?*
The FOREMAN: *All agreed.*
The CORONER: *What is your verdict?*
The FOREMAN: *A verdict of wilful murder against Thomas William Sadler.*
The CORONER: *Then it is my sad duty to commit Thomas William Sadler to take his trial at the Assizes on the charge of 'Wilful murder.'*

Sadler was subsequently brought to trial at the Chelmsford Summer Assize on Wednesday, 29 July 1891 with the case being described by the Judge as the most serious that they had to deal with. The prisoner arrived at the court just before a quarter to eleven. As he was being led into the side entrance of the Shire Hall, he paused for a second or two, and looking round at the large crowd assembled, he exclaimed in a loud voice, 'Goodbye, all of you.' Once inside the courtroom he immediately took his place in the dock. After throwing his fur cap into the corner he gazed around the court, and in particular spent some time looking at those seated in the public gallery.

Having been arraigned and called upon to plead, the prisoner took a piece of paper from his waistcoat pocket, and after familiarising himself with its contents, said, 'I leave it to my solicitor – I wish to have the case proved.' The witnesses for the prosecution were then called to give their evidence. These included Robert Wass, brother of the deceased, whose evidence had not previously been heard. He told the court that after the prisoner had moved out of his brother's home last August, he had gone to live with him for seven or eight weeks. On the night of the stabbing he said that the prisoner had called at his house earlier in the evening and had said that he was not happy about the situation with the children. The witness then related to the court details of the conversation that had taken place:

> He came in about 7.30 in the evening and asked me how the children were getting on. I replied, 'You don't want to ask how they are getting on – four children and no mother!' He replied, 'No, I feel vexed for them. But she left her home for me, or through me. I said it and I'll stick to it – she shall never want for anything, as long as I have a penny, she shall have it. If I can't work for it, I'd rob for it. If I have to suffer and before he [the deceased] should lay a finger on her, I will cut his throat.

The witness then stated that the prisoner seemed quite sensible at the time and did not appear to be any the worse for drink. After the assault had taken place he said that he sat up with his brother whilst he was ill. He said that at one stage he seemed to be getting much better and even came downstairs on the Saturday and Sunday. His hand though had been strapped to his side to prevent him from tearing his wounds open.

At the conclusion of the case for the prosecution, Mr Murphy Q C delivered a powerful address on behalf of the prisoner - his objective being to secure a verdict of manslaughter. He strongly challenged the theory of the prosecution that the prisoner had started out in the morning with the intention of committing murder, and spoke instead of the prisoner's past history which was totally inconsistent with the idea of violence. He concluded by saying that as much as they might disapprove of the conduct of the prisoner, both to the deceased and to his wife, the justice of the country did not require that another life should be forfeited.

His Lordship's summing up of the case, however, was very much in favour of the prosecution. He carefully went through the evidence which had been presented, calling attention to a number of salient points and points of law. With regard to the deceased, he said that he was at a loss to come up with a single angry word, or act of aggression, that he had made towards the prisoner. And he who had intruded into his home for the purpose of robbing him of his children. He could show no circumstance which would justify, or extenuate, the striking of that deadly blow. With reference to the wound itself, he said that even supposing that death had ensued from careless or neglectful treatment, that would in no way lessen the responsibility of the prisoner in the eyes of the law. Throughout the entire length of his summing up, which lasted for nearly an hour, the prisoner was paying rapt attention to what was being said and was visibly straining to hear every word.

Immediately after the summing up had been concluded, the Jury were asked to consider their verdict. Without even leaving their box they had a short huddled discussion, before announcing that they were prepared with their verdict:

The CLERK: *Gentlemen of the Jury, are you agreed upon your verdict?*
The FOREMAN: *We are.*
The CLERK: *Do you find the prisoner at the bar guilty or not guilty?*
The FOREMAN: *Guilty.*
The CLERK: *Of wilful murder?*
The FOREMAN: *Yes, sir.*

The verdict was heard with breathless silence, and whilst the sentence of death was being read out, you could have heard a pin drop. Assuming the black cap, the learned Judge then said:

Thomas William Sadler, you have been convicted of the crime of wilful murder as conclusive as it is possible to conceive. You had robbed the poor dead man, your victim, of his wife. You had availed yourself of the opportunities afforded to you when a lodger in his house of seducing her from his affections. You had placed him in the most miserable condition that a man can be placed, and because of the heartlessness of his wife and her seducer, he was left with four poor little children to be maintained and cared for by him. I do not believe in the professed affection which it is said you entertained for these children. For six whole months after leaving them with their father, never on a single occasion had you shown them kindness or affection, or sought them out. But their mother, for some reason or other, on May 25 decided further to distress the father by taking his children from him, and attempting, through the medium of that woman Johnson, to steal them from him. Having failed in that attempt you had undertaken to do the same thing for her if you could by going to the house of that poor man and robbing him of his children, the only creatures left to him of endearment. And because he did not choose to allow you to take them, you had made up your mind to kill him....

The crime of murder in this country, and by the laws of it, can be expiated by one penalty only – the penalty of death, which I am about to pronounce upon you. I pray you, however, before I perform that solemn and sad duty, to listen to one word of exhortation from me, to make use of the few days that are left to you on this earth in seeking pardon from Almighty God, who alone has power to pardon you your great sin. Your days are numbered. Think no more of this world when you descend the steps of the dock in which you now stand. I can hold out no hope of mercy being extended to you.

The Judge then pronounced the sentence of death upon the prisoner and he was taken from the court. The final decision as to whether the sentence of hanging would actually take place would rest, as always, with the Home Secretary. This decision was always made after taking due note of any recommendations for leniency that may have been made by the court of conviction. As far as the case of Thomas Sadler was concerned, however, the Judge had already hinted that he would not be making any such recommendation, thereby making it extremely unlikely that the Home Secretary would overturn the court's ruling. Even so, the prisoner's legal team did their best to get the sentence commuted to a custodial sentence, by launching an appeal for mercy.

The Home Secretary's decision regarding the appeal for leniency arrived by letter at the office of the prisoner's Colchester solicitors two weeks later:

Whitehall 14th August 1891

Gentlemen, - With reference to your letter of the 11th inst., and other representations on behalf of Thomas William Sadler, now lying under sentence of death for murder, I am directed by Mr Secretary Matthews to acquaint you that, after consultation with the learned Judge before whom the prisoner was tried, and careful consideration of all the circumstances of the case, he regrets that he has failed to discover any sufficient grounds to justify him in advising Her Majesty to interfere with the due course of law.

I am your obedient servant,
Godfrey Lushington

Meanwhile, within the confines of the Convict Prison at Springfield, the condemned man had been saying his last goodbyes to his family and friends. One particularly poignant meeting took place when the prisoner's father paid him a farewell visit. He arrived at Chelmsford by train from Colchester and at once proceeded to the house of Mr H Sorrell, in Railway Square. Although the two men were not related in any way, they had met at the time of the trial and Mr Sorrell had been touched by the old man's trouble and had taken him home with him. And now, on Monday, 17 August, the day before the execution, the two men walked up to the prison. Although Mr Sorrell was not admitted, Mr Sadler enjoyed an unusually long interview with his son. Again and again the prisoner told his father that he was willing and prepared to die, but the poor old man was inconsolable and could not force himself to utter the last goodbye. At length the moment of parting arrived and he left the prison broken-hearted. Speaking later of the time that he spent with his son he admitted that he was in a terrible fix, but seemed to be prepared: 'They would not let us go nearer to each other than I am to that fireplace (about two yards), and some of the keepers were there all the time as we talked to each other through the grating. He said that he was sorry for what he'd done, but he hardly knew what he was about when he done it.'

Later that day, Mr Berry, the executioner, arrived at Chelmsford on the five-fifteen train from his home in Bradford. He was stylishly dressed in a coffee-coloured suit with a dark brown hat, and was carrying a large yellow 'Gladstone' bag with a light coloured cloak slung over his arm. In fact, according to one bystander, he looked more like a publican than an executioner. After taking some refreshment he went straight to the execution chamber and checked that the mechanism was in order.

At seven forty-five the following morning the prisoner ate his last meal consisting of soup, cocoa and an egg. Shortly before eight o'clock Mr Berry arrived at the condemned man's cell and shook him by the hand. He then set about pinioning his arms, an act to which the prisoner quietly submitted, although there was a little quivering of his lips and his face was a deadly shade of pale. The pinioning process consisted of strapping the prisoner's arms to his side, as far down as his elbows, with the forearms being fixed in the horizontal position. The legs were left free at this stage to enable the prisoner to walk to the scaffold.

When the party arrived at the execution chamber (a small room housing the scaffold and twelve foot deep pit) Berry stood the prisoner on the trap door, strapped his legs, pulled a white cap over his head, and whilst the prison Chaplain was still reading some verses of scripture he pulled the lever and launched the prisoner into eternity. The moment the trap door opened Sadler quickly disappeared from view - the rope tightened and the spectators turned pale as they heard the distinctive sound of the prisoner's neck breaking. Sadler had made no statement whatsoever prior to his death, and his demeanour on the scaffold, and indeed throughout the whole painful scene, was described by one of the officials as 'good.' Outside the prison a black flag was unfurled to let the gathered crowd know that the deed had been done.

As a final note to this sorry saga, it may interest readers to know what ultimately happened to the victim's wife and his five children. Well, in less than a year from the time of her lover's execution, Eliza Wass had met and married another man named Thomas Fenner, from Ardleigh, and had been reunited with her four older children. At the time of the 1901 census, Hector Wass (her eldest son who witnessed the assault on his father) was now twenty-two-years-old, married to a girl named Emma, and working as a sawyer's labourer. Ethel and Florence, now aged twenty and eighteen respectively, were both trouser machinists working from home; Archibald, aged fourteen, was working as an agricultural labourer and the baby of the family – Beatrice, who her mother had kept with her, was now twelve-years-old and still at school.

Bromley Road, looking towards the junction with Harwich Road. The former Royal Oak *public house can be seen behind the parked cars. 2005*
The Author

CHAPTER 14

The Colchester Fire Murder
1893

The body was virtually unrecognisable.

One of the most sensational murder cases to have occurred in late Victorian times was the so-called Colchester Fire Murder of 1893. From what at first appeared to be a routine case of fire at the premises of a local tailor, the incident quickly developed into one of arson, robbery and murder of the worst kind. Within a day or so the police were hot on the trail of the man who they believed could help with their inquiries, but in the confusion that ensued in the hours following the event the suspect managed to make good his escape. However, his description and particulars were soon circulated to police forces throughout the country and it would surely be just a matter of time before he was apprehended – or would it? Back in Colchester, the place remained abuzz with excitement for weeks to follow as the case continued to make headline news. Sightings of the fugitive continued to come in from all quarters and the police remained confident that they would soon have their man. But as the weeks and months went on, and with no apparent breakthrough, the case was fast developing into one of the town's greatest mysteries.

The fire at Mr Alfred Welch's tailoring shop, which stood on the corner of Short Wyre Street and St Botolph's Street, was first spotted by Police Constable Charles Alexander who was on duty in the area shortly before ten o'clock on the evening of Friday, 8 December 1893. He had been walking past the premises when he noticed a smell of burning and believing that there was something amiss at the property adjoining Mr Welch's, he decided to investigate. It was while he was looking round this property that he noticed that the upper part of Mr Welch's place was on fire. He at once raised the alarm and directed a man named Strutt to report the matter to the Police Station. Within minutes the turncocks (persons who operated the valves for the main water supply) and members of the Essex and Suffolk and Volunteer Fire Brigades were summoned to the scene. The first to arrive was Fireman Rice of the Volunteer Brigade who immediately burst open the door leading into Short Wyre Street, and after working his way through the building found that most of the upper floors were well alight. By this time the rest of the Volunteer Brigade had arrived with their steam engine, and were immediately followed by the crew of the Essex and Suffolk. As soon as the brigades arrived they lost no time in getting to work and, having found a good supply of water, were soon directing no less than six jets onto the blaze (apparently the force of water from the hydrants was so good that it was not necessary to work the engines).

By this time a large crowd had gathered to watch the progress of the fire as it burnt furiously for a considerable time, before finally being brought under control just before midnight. It was not, however, until past one o'clock in the morning that it was deemed safe enough to investigate the interior of the building. Throughout most of this time the whereabouts of the owner of the shop, Mr Welch, had become the subject of concern. Enquiries had been made at his home in Queen Street as well as at his Club, but he could not be found. As it turned out, one of the firemen working with the Volunteer Brigade was a man named Henry Sizzey, who was employed as a manager by Mr Welch and had been with him earlier in the evening before leaving to go home around eight o'clock. But now, as the firemen made their way through the partially burnt out building, they were to make a gruesome discovery. At the foot of a stairway between the first and second floors of the building they found the charred remains of Mr Welch, lying amid a pile of debris. The body was virtually unrecognisable. The lower limbs had been completely burnt away, as had both of the forearms. The hair and scalp had been almost entirely destroyed and the skull was badly charred and fractured. In fact, the body had only been identified as that of Mr Welch by the discovery of his keys lying underneath the

An artist's impression of the wanted man, Arthur Blatch. Essex Police Museum

body, and the remains of a double truss which Mr Welch was known to have worn. Shortly after the body had been found a rather strange thing happened. Fireman Sizzey apparently rushed over to the body and tried to pick it up. He then became very excited and began to repeat several times that 'Blatch' was a murderer, and that he had killed his master. It was then with great difficulty that he was removed from the building into the street where he continued to shout 'He's a murderer, he's a murderer.' When questioned further about the matter by the Head Constable, Mr R O Coombs, who was also present, he made them aware of an intriguing conversation which he had had with Mr Welch earlier in the evening. He explained how Mr Welch had spent the day in London before arriving back at the shop about seven-thirty in the evening:

When Mr Welch came in he asked me what kind of day I had had. I told him what I had done and after taking a look at the order book he turned to me and said that he had just seen Arthur Blatch, a porter who used to work for him, and that he had said that he wanted to see him privately after everyone had gone. He asked me what I thought he wanted, and I told him that he probably wanted to borrow some money and that he should have nothing to do with him. He then said that Blatch had told him that something terrible was going to happen, or had happened, I can't remember which, and then said that he would look jolly sharp that he didn't get any money from him. I then left the shop with two other employees about eight o'clock and left Mr Welch alone in his office.

Could it be that this Arthur Blatch had in fact entered the building after everyone had gone home and had then robbed and murdered his former employer before setting fire to the building in an attempt to cover up his crime? Or could it be that Sizzey was making the whole thing up? Had he in fact returned to the shop after the others had left and murdered his master before setting fire to the building? For the next forty-eight hours rumours were spreading about the town about Sizzey's possible involvement, while the police were kept busy following up numerous lines of inquiry. In particular, they spent a fair amount of time interviewing witnesses and checking out Sizzey's story. The police had also begun to make inquires at the home of Blatch's estranged wife who lived in Chapel Street and was acting as landlady to a police officer who was lodging with her. However, initial inquiries revealed that Blatch had not been seen in Colchester for some time and was thought to be living at a house in Great Titchfield Street, London, but enquiries by Detective Sergeant Alexander from Colchester Police force, who travelled to London on the Sunday, failed to find any trace of him. In fact, the owner of the

An artist's impression of Alfred Welch's business premises on the corner of St Botolph's Street and Short Wyre Street. Essex Police Museum

Short Wyre Street, looking towards St Botolph's Street. Alfred Welch's place was at the end of the row of buildings on the right. c.1924.
Jess Jephcott

house, a Mrs Elizabeth Lincoln, and Blatch's former landlady, said that he and 'Mrs Blatch' (a woman named Elizabeth Rash) had both left the house about a month previously.

Back in Colchester, on the Sunday afternoon, an initial post-mortem examination was carried out on the deceased's remains by Dr Maybury, the Police Surgeon, and Dr Becker from Queen Street. Of particular interest were the remains of some charred rope which had apparently been found wound round the neck at least two or three times, and which had caused some damage or wounding. The suggestion, of course, was that he may have been strangled, or perhaps may have even attempted to take his own life. As a result of this tentative examination, which lasted for about an hour, it appeared that death had indeed occurred from some form of suffocation, caused either by the smoke from the fire, or from strangulation. At this point it was decided to call a halt to the examination until the assistance of a surgical expert from the Home Office could be secured. Accordingly, Mr Thomas Bond, Surgeon to Westminster Hospital, was sent to Colchester to assist. The three medical officers then collaborated to complete the examination which resulted in some startling new evidence being discovered.

The Adjourned Coroner's Inquest (originally opened on 9 December) was held in the Town Hall on Thursday, 28 December. Mr Bond was the second witness called after the midday break and delivered his evidence from a written statement. The following extract is a condensed version of his evidence:

> *The body was charred by fire, both legs and thighs had been burnt off, and both forearms. The left upper arm was the only part of the body which was uncharred. The features were burnt away and quite unrecognisable. The hair and scalp were entirely destroyed, and the bones of the skull were charred through in places. On the upper and back part of the skull, on the right side, there was extensive fracture of the bones, and just over the right ear the brain was protruding. Around the neck, especially the back part of the neck, there was a deepish groove, an inch and a half in width and half an inch deep. It*

showed the indentation of a rope. The groove was quite low down in the neck, near the shoulders and on a level with the lower part of the larynx. The liver was dried up by the fire; the abdominal walls were very nearly consumed by the fire, and the contents of the abdomen dried up. I then turned out all the brain and all the contents of the skull, and examined the base for fracture. In fact, we all three examined it – Dr Becker and Dr Maybury. We found no fracture. The remarkable thing which we did find was the extensive effusion of blood between the skull cap and the fibrous covering of the brain. I have no doubt that this blood was effused during life, and I have no doubt either that it was caused by extensive fractures of the skull during life. The injuries which I found were quite sufficient to cause death, and also to cause death very quickly. Then again, I am able to say that the death was not caused by strangulation. I have no doubt that the man met his death from violent blows inflicted on the head with a heavy instrument.

Members of the Volunteer Fire Brigade pose for this group photograph outside Colchester castle in 1880. Author's collection

This evidence of Mr Bond finally cleared up a number of uncertainties and confusion which had surrounded the case from the time that the fire had first been discovered. Initially it had been thought that it was an ordinary case of fire, then one of suicide, and now, thanks to the medical evidence, almost certainly one of murder and arson (although robbery was also later added to the crime). It would now appear that whoever was responsible for committing the crime had killed Mr Welch with heavy blows to the head, and had then put a rope around his neck in an attempt to make it look like suicide, before finally setting fire to the building.

Earlier in the day Henry Sizzey had been called to give evidence and when questioned had fully restated his recollection of events, from the time of his conversation with Mr Welch, concerning the intended visit of Blatch, his movements after leaving the shop around eight o'clock, to his eventual return two hours later to assist in fighting the fire. Fortunately for Sizzey his story had been fully substantiated by a number of independent witnesses and the police were now fully satisfied as to his innocence. When questioned further, however, about the character of Arthur Blatch and the conversation which had passed between himself and Mr Welch, he said that Blatch had some two years previously been employed as a porter for Mr Welch and that he had been dismissed for taking too much time off from work on the pretence of being sick. Since that time he believed that Blatch had called on Mr Welch on several occasions for the purpose of borrowing some money, but was unable to say whether or not he had received any. Sizzey did, however, confirm that Mr Welch always kept a sizeable reserve of money in his cash box, which when found by the police and firemen was found to be empty. In fact, earlier in the day, the court had heard evidence from Mr W H Short, a local accountant, who having examined Mr Welch's assortment of cash books and other related papers, was able to confirm that there should have been a cash surplus at the end of trading on 8 December of £95-2s-10d, plus a couple of pounds which had been left over from money set aside for paying the staff wages. All in all, nearly £100 (about £6,500 in today's money) was unaccounted for.

St Botolph's Street, looking north towards Queen Street, about 1912. Note the latest women's fashions hanging outside the shop front and what appear to be gas light fittings hanging over the front of some of the shops. Jess Jephcott

The Coroner now turned his attention to the main suspect of the crime, Alfred Blatch, who according to a few witnesses had been seen in the town on the day of the murder. The main witness to this effect was William Went, a boot and shoe maker, of 10 Sheepen Road who had told police that he had seen Blatch on the night of the murder standing near the Theatre Royal in Queen Street. Here follows part of Mr Went's evidence:

[Note the long drawn out style of questioning.]

The CORONER: *Do you recollect standing near the Theatre?*
Answer: *Yes.*
Question: *About what time?*
Answer: *About ten minutes to eight.*

Question: *Who were you waiting for?*
Answer: *Mr George Scrutton of Roman Road.*
Question: *He works for Mr Berry Halls, bootmaker of North Hill?*
Answer: *Yes.*
Question: *While standing there did you see anybody?*
Answer: *I saw Blatch.*
Question: *Arthur Blatch?*
Answer: *Yes.*
Question: *Who did he used to work for?*
Answer: *Mr Welch.*
Question: *Where was he?*
Answer: *Outside Mr Welch's shop.*
Question: *Near Mr Mence Smith's shop?*
Answer: *No, near Mr Warren's old boot factory.*
Question: *Is that immediately opposite Mr Welch's?*
Answer: *Yes Sir.*
Question: *And adjoins Mr Mence Smith's shop?*
Answer: *Yes.*
Question: *Have you any doubt whatever that it was Arthur Blatch?*
Answer: *No, I have not.*

St Botolph's Street, looking in the direction of Mersea Road, around 1903. Mr Mence Smith's shop seen on the left of the picture, was almost opposite Mr Welch's premises. Jess Jephcott

After another twenty or so questions from the Coroner, all in a similar vein to the above, and confined to eliciting minute details regarding Blatch's precise position in the street etc., it was the turn of the members of the Jury to question the witness:

Mr BEDWELL: *You didn't speak to him?*
Answer: *No.*
Question: *You are positive that you saw him on the night of the fire?*
Answer: *Yes, I am.*
The FOREMAN: *Were you there before Blatch arrived?*
Answer: *Yes.*
Question: *And Blatch came up?*
Answer: *Yes.*
Question: *Which way did he come?*
Answer: *From the direction of Queen Street.*
Question: *Which side?*
Answer: *On the left, the same side as Mr Welch's house.*
Question: *Did he pass by where you were standing?*
Answer: *No, he was on the other side of the road. I was standing against Mr Byford's, directly opposite the Theatre.*
Question: *When you saw him did he appear to come from Queen Street, or as if he came from a house?*
Answer: *He appeared to come straight from Queen Street.*
Question: *Is there any particular reason why you should not have spoken to each other?*
Answer: *Oh, no, no.*
Question: *You were friendly?*
Answer: *Oh, yes, and I believe I should have spoken to him if I had been on the other side. I was waiting for a friend to go to the Theatre.*
The CORONER: *What time did you go to the Theatre?*
Answer: *About two or three minutes to eight.*

And with that the witness was excused. A number of other witnesses were called to testify that they had seen a man enter Mr Welch's shop shortly after eight o'clock. The first of these witnesses called was Martha Green, the wife of William Green, a carman (driver of a cart), of 1 Canterbury Road. She recalled how she had seen somebody enter Mr Welch's shop on the night of the fire as she was returning home:

I recollect the night of the fire on 8 December. I was in Long Wyre Street that evening, near Mr Garlings [baker], when I heard a foundry whistle – it was eight o'clock. I walked straight down Short Wyre Street, in the direction of Mr Welch's shop, and went straight home. When I got near Mr Welch's shop, and on the same side of the street, I saw a man go into the side door of Mr Welch's shop against the office. That would be about five minutes past eight. I saw the man's face, but I did not know him. I do not know Arthur Blatch, but he was of about medium height and was wearing an overcoat and a hard hat.

Two other witnesses, who lived opposite Mr Welch's shop, also testified that they had seen a man leaving the shop about nine thirty and walk up Short Wyre Street towards Eld Lane. They never saw his face but recalled that he was wearing a long overcoat and a hard hat.

A number of other witnesses told the court that they had seen a man answering Blatch's description at various points along the road between Colchester and Witham on the night of the fire. Mr H Ollard, landlord of the *Swan Inn* at Stanway, had said that on the night of the fire he had answered his door to a suspicious looking character sometime around 10.45 pm, who asked him if he would sell him a little brandy. He said that he was going to Kelvedon to catch the morning mail up (train to London), and appeared to be breathing hard as though he had been walking fast. Mr Ollard also stated that the man was wearing a long coat and what appeared to be a black and white checked cap. He said it was difficult to be precise as the man had refused to go inside and had remained on the step, partly in the shadows. He also noted, however, that he was carrying a case, which he took to contain a fishing rod, and a basket.

As the suspect continued his journey along the London Road he was spotted by Police Constable John Isom at Easthorpe Corner, which is about two miles from Kelvedon Railway Station:

It would have been about midnight, or a minute or two afterwards. When I met him he told me that he had just been frightened by somebody in the hedge, and I told him not to worry as it was only another policeman. I could see PC Bright from Marks Tey coming along the road. I asked the man what he was doing and he said that he had come up from Marks Tey and wanted to get on the mail train, but finding that it didn't stop there was going on to Kelvedon. I saw that he was carrying a long case which I took to contain a fishing rod, but he told me that he was a photographer and that the case contained his tripod. With that he bade us both goodnight and we saw no more of him.

Blatch was finally seen by several other witnesses at Witham Railway Station a little after two o'clock in the morning. Thomas Gilbey, a mail cart driver between Maldon and Witham, said that he saw a man carrying a basket come into the station about 2.20 am and who was making enquiries about the mail train:

I said good morning to him and he asked me how long it would be before the mail train left. I told him that it had passed through about ten minutes ago, and he said, 'Oh dear, I wouldn't have missed that train for any money.' He asked me the time of the next train and I told him that I didn't think that there would be another one until seven or eight o'clock in the morning. A goods train happened to pull in at that moment and he asked me if I thought that they would let him on that. I told him that I had never known anyone to get on before, and he said that he didn't mind how much he had to pay as he had a lot of business to do in London.

Some of the porters from the station had also testified that they had seen him counting a lot of money while he was waiting at the station. Blatch was, of course, riding his luck but he succeeded in getting on the 7.48 train for London several hours later. And with that he disappeared into the thronging metropolis. After hearing the evidence of several other witnesses throughout the day, the proceedings were adjourned until Thursday, 11 January 1894.

As it turned out, the police had come within a whisker of capturing Blatch just two days after the murder when they called at his London lodging address for the purpose of issuing him with a summons to appear before the Inquest (at that time there was no evidence of foul play). It may be remembered that Detective Sergeant Alexander had been despatched to London on the Sunday after the fire to enquire as to Blatch's whereabouts at an address in Great Titchfield Street. The landlady of the house, Mrs Elizabeth Lincoln, had told the detective that Blatch had left her house a month ago, but this was now known to be a lie, for Blatch and his female companion, Elizabeth Rash, were actually inside the house at the time watching events from a window. After being tipped off that the police were looking for him, both he and Rash fled the house in a cab the following day.

Elizabeth Lincoln had since been interviewed several times by the police and was one of the main witnesses in attendance at the reconvened inquest. She was accused of deliberately trying to mislead the police, but responded by saying that it must have been her daughter who gave the false information. And when pressed on the point, and a number of other matters, she remained as non-committal as she possibly could and had to be reminded of the consequences of telling an untruth. In fact, at the conclusion of the proceedings the Coroner made a special point of stating that she had given her evidence in a most unsatisfactory manner, and he thought that it was due to her that Blatch was not there to answer the charge of the wilful murder of Mr Welch.

Following the departure of Blatch and Rash from the Great Titchfield Street address on Monday, 11 December, the police were eventually able to trace Rash to a house in Harrow Road where she was living with her sister. Blatch was not with her, but after being taken by police to Scotland Yard she co-operated fully with the investigating officers. And now, her appearance at court, along with that of Mrs Lincoln, caused a sensation as she was called to give evidence. Here follows a condensed version of her testimony to the court:

The CORONER: *How long have you known Arthur Blatch?*
Answer: *About four years.*
Question: *He is a married man?*
Answer: *Yes. I left Colchester with Arthur Blatch about two years ago, and we went to live at 355 City Road, London. We lived there about nine months and from there we went to Mrs Lincoln's, Great Titchfield Street. Blatch was then working as a porter at the Scotch Stores in Oxford Street.*
Question: *Did he leave?*
Answer: *He left that situation in April or June 1893, and set up as a photographer. He hired a camera from the National Photo Company of 82 Bishopsgate Street.*
Question: *When did you leave Mrs Lincoln's?*
Answer: *We left Mrs Lincoln's some time around the 9 June and went to Plymouth, where he was agent for the Company, going around taking photos and teaching photography. We returned to Great Titchfield Street on 23 October. After we returned Blatch did not do anything for a living, and he left me at Mrs Lincoln's on 10 November to come to Colchester. When he left he owed about three weeks rent, I think. He did not give me any money before leaving.*
Question: *Did he tell you whether he was getting behind or in any trouble?*
Answer: *No, but he had no money when he left, only tuppence.*
Question: *He was very hard up?*
Answer: *Yes.*
Question: *When did you see him again?*
Answer: *I did not see him again until he came home on Saturday, 9 December, between ten and eleven in the morning.*

The Coroner then asked the witness numerous questions regarding the clothing that Blatch was wearing when he arrived home and also whether she could identify a small black and white checked cap which had been recovered from her London address. She remembered seeing it when he took it from his coat pocket after arriving home on the Saturday morning. (It may be remembered that the man who called at the *Swan Inn* at Stanway on the night of the fire was wearing such a cap, and that the same cap had since been identified as belonging to one of Mr Welch's employees who had left it in the shop on the night of the murder). The witness had also told the court that Blatch had been wearing a new set of clothes when he returned home, and that she had asked him whether he had got them from Mr Welch.

The CORONER: *When you mentioned Mr Welch's name did you notice anything?*
Answer: *Yes, he turned very white, and sat down on the bed.*
Question: *Did he say how he got home from Colchester?*
Answer: *He said that he walked from Colchester to Witham.*
Question: *Did he tell you of anything that happened on the way?*
Answer: *No, nothing, only that he rode by train from Witham to Stratford, and then took the tram to Whitechapel.*
Question: *When he came home did he give you any money?*
Answer: *He gave me £1.*
Question: *Did you see any more money?*
Answer: *Yes, after dinner he took out from his trouser pocket two or three packages of money wrapped up in newspaper.*
Question: *What did he do with that?*
Answer: *He counted it on the table.*
Question: *What did it consist of?*
Answer: *Sovereigns and half sovereigns.*
Question: *What did he do when he had finished counting the money?*
Answer: *He put it back in his pocket.*
Question: *Did you see how much gold there was?*
Answer: *About £80.*
Question: *Was Blatch in the house when Alexander first came?*
Answer: *Yes, he was.*
Mr JONES: *You say that it was between one and two when Alexander called on the Sunday. Could Blatch see Alexander?*
Answer: *Yes, because he was looking at him out of the window. After that Mrs Lincoln had a conversation with him.*

The Coroner then proceeded to sum up the evidence presented to the Jury. He made particular reference to the evidence given by Elizabeth Rash who had confirmed that Blatch had indeed travelled to Colchester some weeks previously. And then there was the evidence of Mr Went who had positively sworn that he had seen Blatch standing opposite Mr Welch's place just before eight o'clock on the night in question. There was also the strong testimony of Mr Ollard from the *Swan Inn*, and also that from the porters at Witham Station, all of whom were agreed that the photograph of Blatch was the same as the man who they had seen counting a large sum of money, and who was in a desperate hurry to get to London. The Coroner finally remarked that in the unlikely event that Blatch was innocent, he had had ample opportunity to come forward and to give an account of himself, but had not done so, and he then asked the Jury to consider their verdict.

The CORONER: *Gentlemen of the Jury, are you agreed upon your verdict?*
The FOREMAN: *We are. The unanimous verdict of the Jury is that the death of Mr Alfred Welch occurred at his place of business, 1 St Botolph's Street, on the evening of Friday, December 8. That it was caused by violent blows to the head, and that such blows were inflicted by Arthur Blatch, against whom they return a verdict of Wilful Murder.*

There was a momentary pause in the courtroom before there came a resounding round of applause, which was difficult to quell. As news of the verdict filtered to the large crowd waiting outside, a similar display of emotion was experienced, which was clear evidence of the high esteem in which the murdered man had been held by all classes in the Borough.

In the normal run of events, the duty of the Coroner would now be to commit the prisoner to appear before the next Assize court to answer for his crime. But Arthur Blatch, of course, was still at large despite extensive efforts by the police to track him down. Hundreds of posters containing a portrait and description of the suspect had been circulated throughout the country, as well as on the continent, and a reward of £50 (about £3,000 today) had been offered by Colchester Police for any information which would lead to his arrest. The description of Blatch which was included on the wanted poster read as follows:

Age about 36; height, 5ft 8in, or 5ft 9in; complexion, pale; eyes, dark and small; moustache, dark brown, may be shaven; face thin, cheeks hollow; thin build; cartilage of throat, or 'Adam's Apple' very prominent; is a great smoker and teeth are discoloured; has suffered from an injury to the spine and frequently stoops a little when walking; his left foot was sprained some years ago, and it occasionally causes light lameness; is fond of bagatelle and fishing; when seen on December 9 was wearing a new black over coat with velvet collar, black and white mixture suit, new lace boots, and black hard hat; he may assume the name of Jackson; has recently been ill, and may affect illness again and remain in bed for a time; it is thought that he is now in hiding at some private lodgings; for the last two years he has worked as a potman, and has travelled the country taking cheap photographs with a self-acting camera.

In the weeks that followed the outcome of the Coroner's proceedings, reports and sightings of Blatch came in from all quarters, including some saying that he had committed suicide, while others were saying that he had been captured. On one occasion a man actually confessed to the crime but was found to have no connection with it. As time went on reports were received that Blatch had been spotted in such faraway places as America, Greece and Australia, but all leads were to prove fruitless. It seemed as though Blatch had literally vanished into thin air. And then nearly seven years later there came the sensational news that Blatch had been spotted and arrested in Auckland, New Zealand.

Back in Colchester, the place was again abuzz with excitement as news continued to trickle through that the New Zealand Police were positive that they had the right man. The man being held in custody, and who was known by the name of Charles Lilleywhite, had been identified as being Arthur Blatch by two or three former Colchester residents. The Colchester Borough Police wasted little time in arranging for him to be brought back home, and they despatched Police Sergeant Frost, who knew Blatch well, and Mr Marsh, the town hall keeper, who had been in the habit of spending holidays with Blatch. The New Zealand Police were as sure as they could be that they had the right man, and so based on their confidence the two men made ready to sail at the earliest opportunity, at an estimated cost to the Borough of between £300-400 (say £25,000 today!).

Several weeks later the all important cable was received from New Zealand bearing the coded message 'Magnet Muddle.' The first word meant, 'Both officers are well and identify Blatch positively. The second word meant, 'Prisoner still denies being Blatch.' But as far as the Colchester Police were concerned, it could equally have stood for 'Total chaos' – as will shortly be revealed! But tension mounted back home as they waited for Lilleywhite to arrive in England. Rumours had spread around the town that his hair had turned grey through the mental strain, and that he was in danger of going insane. He had, also, apparently on several occasions answered to the name of Blatch, and yet, photographs of the man showed him to be of a somewhat larger build than Blatch, although there was a marked facial resemblance.

On Sunday, 16 June 1901, seven and a half years after the crime was committed, Lilleywhite arrived in England and was immediately transported by train to Colchester where he appeared before the Borough court. A journalist who had travelled on the same train reported that the man in custody was of medium size, with dark hair turning grey, nose straight and well formed, eyes a dull brown with bushy eyebrows, ears rather prominent and set at an angle from the head. His complexion was also said to contain visible faint pittings of smallpox, which was a point in his favour as there was evidence that Charles Lilleywhite, the man who he was claiming to be, had suffered from smallpox.

After arriving in the town, the prisoner was taken to the court to appear before the Borough magistrates where he was charged with the wilful murder of Mr Welch. The prisoner, after having waved his hand in recognition to Mr Isaac Lilleywhite from Leeds (who he professed to be his brother) then stated in a clear voice:

'My name is not Arthur Blatch. It never has been, and it never will be.' He then challenged anyone in the court to prove the contrary (applause).

Lilleywhite then continued to address the court:

> *I understand the position thoroughly, but the point is this. I understand that in the British nation, or in a part of the world where the English language is spoken, a man is presumed innocent until he has been proven guilty. It has not been proved that I am Arthur Blatch, and you have a mighty job in hand to prove it. I think it is only just that I should be allowed to wear my own name until it is proved otherwise* [applause].

The MAYOR: *So far as this court is concerned you stand before us as Arthur Blatch, and we do not know you by any other name, until you have proved yourself to be somebody else.*
PRISONER: *I have to prove my innocence and you have to prove my guilt.*

The prisoner was then remanded in custody to appear before the court at a later date. On the following Tuesday morning, several men of middle age, average height and with dark greying hair were in great demand as the police assembled a line up of people to take part in an identification parade. A number of witnesses, who had stated that they would know Blatch anywhere, were invited to inspect the line-up, which included the man from New Zealand. Among them were Mr Sizzey, Mr Welch's former manager, Mr Hatherley, another employee, Mr Page of West House Farm, Fingringhoe, Mr Gates of Priory Street and a lady known as Margaret Archer. The identification test was carried out in private, but as the day went on the impression that a grave mistake had taken place was slowly gathering momentum. In fact, most of the witnesses who saw the prisoner were of the opinion that the man in custody was not Blatch.

The final stage in this dramatic sequence of events took place on Wednesday, 26 June when the suspect Lilleywhite was brought before the court to answer the charges brought against him. Lilleywhite appeared perfectly calm and sat with his arms folded as the story of the crime was unfolded by Mr Graham Campbell, barrister, who was acting on behalf of the Director of Public Prosecutions. Mr Campbell said that although there was undoubtedly a most remarkable resemblance between Lilleywhite and Blatch, the evidence of identity was such that would not justify a further remand. He then amazed the court by asking that the prisoner be immediately discharged from custody. Obviously a dramatic blunder had taken place. It had apparently been proved beyond doubt that Mr Lilleywhite was exactly who he claimed to be, resulting in a terrible case of mistaken identity which only added to the whole 'comedy of errors', which seemed to have blighted this case from start to finish.

The Mayor accordingly discharged Lilleywhite but he seemed reluctant to leave the court, as he wanted to ask questions of the witnesses who had been responsible for him being brought here (remember that Lilleywhite was fighting his corner single handed). In particular, he wanted to question Police Sergeant Frost who had travelled to New Zealand to arrest him, and who had been waiting outside the court ready to give evidence against him. The bench consented to Sergeant Frost being questioned and he was subsequently called to the witness box and questioned by Lilleywhite. Frost insisted that there was indeed a strong resemblance, but said that he had not identified him in the first instance because he (Lilleywhite) was wearing a massive beard. Lilleywhite then asked if he could call Margaret Archer. 'That lady has been the cause of all this trouble, and I should like to ask her a few questions,' he said. However, after being consulted by court officials, she said that she did not want to give evidence, and would only do so under compulsion.

So a very unhappy Lilleywhite had no option but to leave the court. He was an American citizen and had wisely placed the matter in the hands of the American Ambassador in London, who in turn had communicated with his government in Washington, as well as with the British government. In a later interview, Lilleywhite said, 'It is a terrible thing for an innocent person to find himself charged with such a crime. I was taken away from my work, carried more than halfway round the globe, held in prison for four months, confined in a hot cabin on a ten week voyage, and suffered untold humiliation and distress.'

Within a short period of time, and having received nothing in the way of a formal apology from the police or from the courts, Lilleywhite sailed home to New Zealand, following the same route that he had previously made as a prisoner of two police officers. He was given a free passage and a cheque for £600 (about £40,000 in today's money) by way of compensation. In their desperation to solve the case, the police and courts had come within a whisker of condemning an innocent man to the gallows – which would only have compounded this terrible crime. And as for Blatch – well he was never heard of again and apparently succeeded in getting away with murder. And as for the reward of £50 offered for information leading to his arrest, well it is probably still outstanding and waiting to be claimed.

A modern-day view of the site where Alfred Welch was murdered. 2005.
The Author

CHAPTER 15

Death in a Sandpit
1926

A man's life had been extinguished in...
a few moments' carelessness...

Before the age of modern health and safety legislation, accidents at work were rife and in many respects considered as par for the course - an acceptable risk that went with the job. When accidents did occur investigators often came to the conclusion that it was all down to bad luck on the part of the individual concerned, rather than apportion too much blame on the employer – who had probably neglected to ensure the safety of his workers in the first place. Of course, serious accidents were always investigated by the local courts, but regardless of their findings, adequate compensation for the victims, or indeed their bereaved families, was virtually unheard of and people were expected to struggle on the best that they could.

One such case in this category occurred on Monday, 22 March, 1926 in the outlying district of Old Heath, when local man Ernie Crick was killed whilst working in a sandpit. The local press covered the story under headlines such as 'Gravel Pit Tragedy at Colchester' and reported the proceedings of the Coroner's inquest which recorded a verdict of accidental death. The owner of the pit, Herbert Berry from the Old Heath Steam Laundry, was cleared of any blame for the incident despite admitting that he had taken little interest in the workings of the pit, after having entrusted all responsibility for the site to his foreman. But to be fair, Mr Berry was simply following in the tracks of many before him who had taken advantage of the extensive deposits of sand and gravel which lay beneath much of Colchester and the surrounding area. It was a sure-fire way of making money during a time of intensive house building in the area following the end of the Great War, as well as providing employment for several local men. But it

Ernie Crick in his army uniform from the First World War.
Sandra Yeomans

was hard work, all carried out by hand, and by the very nature of the exercise (i.e. working directly beneath tons of unstable material) a high risk occupation.

But as Ernie and his work colleague Fred Johnson toiled away in the pit on that cold Monday afternoon, they never for a moment expected disaster to strike. This is not to say that they were entirely ignorant of the risks involved. On the contrary, when working at the bottom of the pit, beneath a thirty foot sloping bank of sand and gravel, they would always have kept one eye alert for minor falls of loose stones and soil which were always coming down, ever ready to scramble clear if necessity arose. But on this particular occasion, when the earth started to move, they failed to get out of the way quickly enough, or at least Ernie Crick did, with devastating consequences as two tons of sand and earth fell on top of him.

At the Inquest held later in the week in the office of the

Fred Johnson (pictured here aged sixty-five) made a valiant attempt to rescue his friend.
Janet Read

Borough Coroner, Mr H Geoffrey Elwes, the deceased was formerly identified as Ernest Crick, a single man aged thirty-nine years who lived at 60 Old Heath with his elderly parents and invalid sister. He had served with the Essex Regiment during the First World War and had been taken prisoner. And although he had only been working at the pit for about five months, he had done similar work before, and prior to the war had also been in Mr Berry's employ. The first witness called was the deceased's friend Frederick Johnson, aged twenty-four years, who gave his account of

what happened. He said that on the Monday afternoon they
had been working at the bottom of the pit in a hole four feet
deep and six feet square when he heard some sand roll down
the face of the pit. Looking upwards he saw a crack and
shouted, 'Look out!' as he jumped clear. But before Ernie
could make his escape a fall of earth and sand had caught him
by his legs. As Johnson hurried to help get him out, another fall
of earth, which included some heavy loam, hit him around the
face and neck and almost completely covered him. Within a
few minutes several other workers employed on the site had
rushed to help Johnson try to get Crick's head clear so that he
could breathe.

Charles Burr, foreman of the site, was the next witness called
and said that he had been working at the top of the pit, some
distance away when the accident occurred. He said that he had
heard a voice and then saw the earth falling. He shouted to
Crick, 'Jump out, Ernie.' But Crick replied, 'I can't,' and he
concluded that he must have been trapped by his legs. By the
time that he had got down to the bottom of the pit the second
fall of earth had occurred and he found Johnson trying to help
his colleague. Dr J R Hickinbotham, who was called to the
scene, said that when he arrived Crick was still partly covered
with several men struggling to get him out. He said that the
deceased was quite dead when they got him out and that an
examination of the body showed that death had been due to
suffocation. The Coroner, at this point, asked if the deceased

*Part of a newspaper report of
the gravel pit tragedy.*
Author's collection

Gravel Pit Tragedy at Colchester

DEATH FROM SUFFOCATION.

The sad story of the death of a gravel-pit
worker, Ernest Crick, aged 39 years, a single
man, of 60, Old Heath, Colchester, was revealed
at an inquest on Wednesday at the offices of
the Borough Coroner (Mr. H. Geoffrey Elwes).
The sole support of his parents, and also of an
invalid sister, deceased was a strong and virile
worker at the gravel pit at 'Old Heath, belonging to Mr. Herbert Berry, of the Old Heath
Steam Laundry, and he lost his life through
the unexpected fall of sand and lumps of loam
while at work with another man.   In the
great war deceased joined up in the Essex
Regiment and served in France. He was for
some time a prisoner of war.

was a strong man. The doctor replied that he was a finely built man, but that in the upright position in which he was trapped the pressure on the body would have been very great.

In closing the proceedings the Coroner said that he had visited the pit the previous afternoon and thought that it appeared to be safer than many he had seen. He found that the cause of death was due to suffocation caused by a fall of loam, following the blowing away of the underlying sand. He said that it was always easy to be wise after the event, but he thought that it might have been better to slope the side of the pit a little more – it struck him as being a little perpendicular, but he would not have been afraid to work in it himself. After hearing that the deceased was the sole support of his aged parents and invalid sister, and hearing that they had no old age pension other than a health benefit allowance, the court simply made their expressions of sympathy to the deceased's relatives. And with that the case was closed. A man's life had been extinguished in what may be described as a few moments' carelessness, and a serious lack of attention to health and safety.

Some sixty-three years after this tragic event had unfolded the author was able to speak with Fred Johnson, who was then in his eighty-eighth year. But time had not dulled his senses or memory of the occasion as he recounted in detail the events which led up to the day in question:

> I remember that Ernie and I had found ourselves out of work and upon hearing that Mr Berry was thinking of starting up a pit near to his laundry, we managed to get taken on. All the ground had to be cleared first – trees had to be cut and old sheds removed – before we could make a start of digging the pit. There was also loads of earth which had to be cleared off the top before we could get to the sand, but we ended up with a thirty foot face. When we got to the bottom we could only go down a few feet further before it filled up with water. We used to get that few feet out all the way along and then go to the top and drop some of the dirt from the top (which we called kaller) down into the water. This would then get washed away and we would then repeat the exercise again and again.

This 1930s view of Old Heath Laundry is seen from the south side of Distillery Pond. The sand pit where Ernie Crick lost his life was a short distance to the right of the laundry building. The laundry was badly damaged by enemy bombing during the Second World War and its replacement has only recently been demolished to make way for modern housing. Author's collection

Well it was one very windy day in March and we were working down in this hole again, getting the sand out ready to put some of this kaller in, when Ernie said to me, 'What do you keep looking up there for Fred?' I said, 'I don't know – them stones keep rattling down and I don't like to hear them.' By the time that a stone had started at the top and rolled down to the base, there was about a quarter of a peck (approx. 9 litres) come down. It was about a quarter to five in the afternoon and I happened to be looking up there and I shouted, 'Look out Ernie', and I could see the face cracking all the way down. I was able to put my hands up to the side and jump out. I was younger than Ernie – he tried to follow me but it came down and caught him round by his legs – that was the first fall, the sand and stuff underneath. Well he twisted round and he could see this big lump coming – because as the bottom fell away the stuff on top would follow soon after. It doesn't come immediately, but it is just behind, and that is where all the kaller was you see, and it came down right on top of him. He was completely buried but I knew just where his head was so we all got round there and scrapped and got his head clear so that he could breathe. I then ran down for Mr Berry and he came up with some brandy and a glass, phoned for the doctor and phoned for the police. We were still trying to dig him out when the doctor arrived – the police didn't come until eight o'clock at night. I was still in Berry's house then because they didn't want me to go home alone. When we'd got poor old Ernie out they laid him on a truck and they took him into the garage and they laid him there all night. The doctor had declared him dead and I remember them giving me some brandy to help calm my nerves. It was the first drop of brandy that I had tasted in my life – it really shook me and I never went back to work for a fortnight.

CHAPTER 16

The Riddle of the Fingringhoe Skeleton
1939

...not one single person had noticed her.

During the last few days of March 1949 the rural peace and quiet of the small village of Fingringhoe, on the outskirts of Colchester, was broken by the arrival of teams of police investigators and Fleet Street crime reporters. The reason for their sudden interest in this rather quiet rural backwater was the discovery of a human skeleton in a small cottage in the centre of the village.

The skeleton was thought to be the remains of Connie Kent, an elderly resident of the village who had mysteriously vanished some ten years previously. In fact, most people in the community had simply assumed that she gone away without telling anyone (as was her custom), and despite some early concerns about her whereabouts, and one or two brief searches made of her small cottage, everyone had simply got on with their lives and forgotten all about her. But now she was the centre of attention; the whole country was talking about her (the story was even run in the *New York Herald Tribune*!) and the village had been catapulted onto the front pages of several national newspapers. But could this really be Connie Kent? And, if so, how long had she been there? How had she met her death? Had she been taken ill and been unable to summon help? Had she died from natural causes? Or had she perhaps suffered at the hands of some violent intruder? These were the kind of questions being asked by the investigating policemen, although they were struggling to find answers. Whatever the truth of the matter it does seem incredulous that her body could have remained unnoticed for such a long period of time, even though her cottage had stood just yards away from the local pub, village school and parish church. Perhaps even more astonishing is the fact that despite numerous individuals having actually been inside the cottage since her disappearance (including police officers, council officials and schoolchildren), not one single person had noticed her.

In the end, it was probably a combination of reports of children breaking into the cottage and efforts by the local authority to have the building demolished, that finally led to the gruesome discovery. Apparently, local parishioners had been complaining about the state of the tumbledown cottage because it had become something of an eyesore in the village. The local council, for their part, were determined to serve a demolition order on the property and had made yet another visit to the cottage in an attempt to make contact with the owner. As they edged their way through the partially open back door of the building they were confronted by a scene that could have been taken straight from the set of the *Marie Celeste* story. There were signs that a meal had been prepared many years earlier, but had not been eaten. A book of Shakespeare's plays was lying open beside a paraffin lamp and there was a pair of slippers by the fireplace. Concerned by what they had seen the officers reported the matter to the police who made arrangements for the property to be properly searched.

The official reports of the case are a little confusing as to exactly what happened next, particularly with regard to the precise sequence of events. However, according to the deputy Coroner's report, one of the first people to examine the cottage was Police Sergeant T Waylett of West Mersea who said that he had found the building to be in a very dilapidated condition with everything in disorder. In the small upstairs bedroom (which measured about 14 feet x 6 feet), he said that he saw a large number of bones which appeared to contain a human leg bone and a skull.

By this time, of course, the press had got wind of the story and had taken up residence at the nearby *Whalebone* public house. The job of leading the investigation for the police had been assigned to Detective Superintendent George Totterdell, head of Essex CID, who together with Detective Inspector George Kemp from Colchester, decided to carry out a detailed examination of the crime scene. However, by the time they had arrived at the cottage, the place had become overrun with reporters, all busy searching for their own clues. Faced with such a commotion, the Superintendent decided that it would probably be best to withdraw for the time being and to return at a later date. On the face of it this seems a little strange. Why on earth didn't he simply order them to leave the building – after all they could have been destroying vital evidence. Writing about the occasion some years later, he had this to say on the matter:

> *The journalists were swarming over the premises and had made their headquarters in the public house opposite. They were convinced that a story was about to break, and each reporter had determined to be the first one in at the death. As soon as I arrived I saw that it was useless starting any serious attempt to investigate with all that crowd around. I returned to my headquarters and later set out again for Fingringhoe in the small hours of the morning, when the bright boys of the press were fast asleep in bed.*

The thatched cottage in the foreground served for many years as a shoe repair shop, and for some time as a doctor's surgery. Connie Kent's cottage, complete with small extension, can be seen to the right of the picture. c.1914. Daphne Allen

THE WHALEBONE CORNER. FINGRINGHOE.

Inside the cottage they found piles of old letters and other correspondence which had built up over the years, as well as a number of photographs of the late Connie Kent, many showing her in theatrical dress – she had apparently once worked as a music hall actress using the stage name Vera Verchayle. In the bedroom they noticed that the bed, although covered in fallen debris from the collapsed ceiling, was still made up and had not been slept in. And lying partially buried beneath a pile of debris in a narrow space between the bed and washbasin, they uncovered what amounted to be a complete human skeleton, still containing remnants of rotting clothing. At this stage, Totterdell decided to call in the local pathologist to help with the investigation. Slowly, but surely, they carried out a fingertip search of the entire room until they were satisfied that they had not missed anything of importance. The skull itself was found to still contain a few tufts of hair which later were matched with some combings found on a hair brush on the dressing table. The skeleton was finally removed to London for analysis where it was examined by Dr Francis Camps, the Home Office pathologist. He found that the skull was still adhered to the neck bones, and that the neck had not been broken. The spine and ribs had been partially eaten away and there was evidence of some arthritis of the spine. He also concluded that the body had been lying on its left side with the right arm slightly raised and dislocated from the shoulder. But no evidence was found to suggest as to how the poor woman had actually met her end – or indeed even if the remains were those of Connie Kent. In a statement to the local press Superintendent Totterdell simply said: 'It may be that she collapsed and died a natural death, but of course we cannot rule out the possibility of foul play.'

This badly faded image of Connie Kent shows her as a young woman around 1900.
Daphne Allen

What was making the investigation even more difficult was the fact that Connie Kent (full name Ada Constance Kent) had become something of a recluse in the village and seldom mixed with others. Very little was known of her past other than the fact that she had been born in the village in 1871 before disappearing from the scene a few years later. In fact, nothing more was heard of her until she returned there in 1928 and took possession of Church Cottage. Witness statements collected from villagers painted a picture of a rather eccentric elderly woman who walked with a stoop, had long dark hair and slightly protruding front teeth. She was also obviously hard of hearing and used to make use of an ear trumpet when speaking with anyone. One of the last people to have seen her alive was Alfred Hasler, the landlord of the *Whalebone* pub, who said that she would come into his place on most days to buy her Woodbine cigarettes. He remembered that he had last seen her on 6 March 1939 when he thought that she had looked very ill and had a violent cold. In fact, when he first came to realise that she was missing from her cottage he went to the trouble of contacting a known friend of hers, a Mrs Maskell from Colchester who, along with a neighbour, went to her cottage to see if she was there. Although they could find no trace of her, or any clue as to where she might be, they failed to alert anyone to the fact as she was in the habit of going off for long periods without telling anyone. No-one quite knew where she used to go but she did apparently have a bit of a temper on her and Mrs Maskell was worried that she might fly at her when she returned if she interfered. Some time later Mrs Maskell returned to the cottage with her son George, to have another look for her, this time actually gaining access to the property, but again finding no sign of her. Finally, towards the end of 1939, or early in 1940, George Wyncoll, a neighbour of Miss Kent, had told the local police that children had been inside the building, and was asking if it could be made secure. When he and the policemen went inside the cottage to have a look round everything appeared to be as normal. They even looked in the bedroom and noted that everything appeared to be tidy, and as far as they could see nobody was there – although they did later admit to having only taken a cursory glance inside the bedroom door.

This was indeed a mystery. If Connie Kent's body had been in the house at the time of all these inspections, and notwithstanding the state that her decomposing body must have been in, surely they could not have failed to notice her. And what about the scores of children who are known to have been inside the cottage over the years – surely they must have seen something? Well one of them apparently did spot some bones but failed to mention it to anyone thinking that they were of no importance. This was Derrick Allen, a local lad from the village, who during the early years of the war, when he was about twelve years old, used to play around inside the cottage with his some of his friends. One of the boys later told the police that he had seen what he believed was a pile of old rags, or clothes, under the bed, whilst Allen was sure that he had spotted some bones on the bedroom floor but thought that a dog must have taken them there. John Hedges was another lad who used to regularly play around the cottage:

> *I often went to explore this wonderful Aladdin's cave where old papers, photographs and books were lying about all over the place. The ground floor was a complete shambles with broken furniture, dislodged bricks, cobwebs and dust covering everything. Thinking back, it's strange to think that nobody ever noticed the body lying there but, like me, they probably never ventured beyond the lower floor of the building.*

And even more tantalising were the rumours that other children from the nearby school had also been inside the cottage and had actually seen Miss Kent lying under the bed. The headmistress of the school, Miss Ethel Donnan, had apparently told detectives that she remembered one day in January 1940 some children coming to her and complaining of a terrible smell coming from the cottage. Suspecting that there might be rats around she contacted the local authorities who went to investigate, but could find no sign of any vermin. It is not known whether they went to the trouble of inspecting the first floor bedroom, and of course they may not have

John Hedges as a seventeen-year-old army recruit. Just a few years earlier he had been a regular visitor to Connie Kent's dilapidated cottage.

John Hedges

The **Whalebone Inn** *and adjacent thatched cottages. Connie Kents's cottage can just be seen to the far right of the picture. Note also the horse-drawn milk cart outside the pub door. c.1910* Fingringhoe Historical Recorders Group

considered any strange smell coming from the building as being anything out of the ordinary, given their line of work. Even closer to the mark was the occasion when a number of the girls had complained about the boys teasing them and warning them not to go into the cottage because Miss Kent was lying dead under the bed – they had apparently seen her hair. Nothing was done to either confirm or deny the rumours and the girls were merely told not to be so silly as the boys were only trying to frighten them.

Although the Coroner's jury returned an Open Verdict when they convened at Witham later in the year, and were of the opinion that the remains were indeed those of Connie Kent, many questions remained unanswered. For example, although there was no evidence of foul play, and most forms of poisoning could be excluded, the real cause of death was unknown. Assuming, therefore, that the remains were those of Connie Kent, why did nobody spot her lying there? Unless, of course, she was not actually there when the searches took place. What if Connie had decided to embark upon one of her frequent trips away from the village and had slipped away from the area unseen? Then, perhaps several months later, after the searches of the cottage had taken place, had returned again in like manner. It may have been then that she was taken ill or met with an accident. By this time most people would have assumed that she had left the village and with the War on had more pressing things on their minds to worry about. On the other hand, of course, she may indeed have been lying there all the time unnoticed. Perhaps she had taken to her bed to lie down after feeling unwell and then fell to the floor as she tried to get up. Could she have dislocated her shoulder at this time and in her attempts to raise herself, or summon help, had rolled partially under the bed and out of view from the door of the room? One other possibility, of course, is that the body did not belong to Connie Kent at all, and could have been the remains of an unknown stranger who for one reason or another had found themselves taking shelter in what they perceived to be a derelict cottage. Connie herself may simply have wandered off to some unknown destination and died there unknown to anyone. With so many people moving around the

Detective Superintendent George Totterdell, who was in charge of the Connie Kent inquiry. Anonymous - The Autobiography of Superintendent G Totterdell (1956)

country during the early years of the War, such an occurrence may not have raised too many suspicions.

Before we close the final curtain on the Connie Kent mystery, perhaps a few words regarding some of the various rumours surrounding her past life may be of interest. Information gleaned from numerous people interviewed at the time of the case suggested that during the 1890s she may have worked as a music hall actress. Another informant said that he was told by Connie herself that she had been one of the original suffragettes who chained themselves to the railings outside the Houses of Parliament. Others had mentioned that she was from a cultured background, was well educated and had travelled widely in her younger days. The photographs of her found in the cottage certainly depicted a well-groomed, good looking woman. Unfortunately there is virtually no surviving evidence of her movements from about the age of twenty until shortly before she moved to Fingringhoe when she was in her late fifties.

What we do know, however, is that Connie was the illegitimate child of Helen Ann Kent who was born at Wivenhoe in 1847. Her grandmother was Fingringhoe-born Mary Ann Kent (neé Jennings) who was married to Joseph Kent, a local sea captain. By the time that Connie was born in 1871 her grandfather had died and shortly thereafter the family, consisting of daughter, mother and grandmother, moved to Shrubland Road in Colchester. At the time of the 1881 census Connie was described as a nine-year-old scholar (suggesting that she was being educated) whilst her mother was employed as a tailoress – presumably for one of Colchester clothing factories. At the time of the 1891 census the family were still living in Shrubland Road although both Connie (now nineteen years old) and her mother were both now described as being dressmakers. No hint yet of a stage career or any involvement with women's suffrage movements. Her mother eventually married George Julius Jarman, a local engineer, in 1898 at the age of forty-nine. From here on little is known of the family's movements apart from the fact that the grandmother was living at the same residence as her son-in-law George Jarman at the time of the 1901 census. She died a few years later in 1904 at the ripe old age of eighty-eight and is buried in Colchester cemetery. However, no trace could be found in the census of either Connie or her mother – they had seemingly vanished from the face of the earth. Searches through local directories and electoral registers have also drawn a blank and it was not until February 1928 that Connie reappears in the official record at Wivenhoe. She was living at the time with a Mrs Emily Davies at Vine Cottage, on the Quayside, and had written a letter to Lexden and Winstree

The Whalebone *public house in 2005.* The Author

Rural District Council asking them what repairs would be necessary to make the Fingringhoe cottage habitable as she wished to live there. By January of 1929 she had apparently taken illegal possession of the cottage, much to the annoyance of council officials who, for whatever reason, decided against pursuing the matter. Following the discovery of her body in 1949 her remains were buried in a Coggeshall churchyard, in what was purported to be a family grave, although no family connections in that area have been uncovered. This is where the story must come to a end – Connie Kent's living years appear to have been just as mysterious as those occasioned by her death.

Index

Index entries in **bold** text indicate references included in illustrations